Change and the Muslim World

Edited by
Philip H. Stoddard,
David C. Cuthell,
Margaret W. Sullivan

Published in cooperation with
The Washington Center of the Asia Society,
The Middle East Institute, and
The National Committee to Honor the Fourteenth Centennial of Islam

SYRACUSE UNIVERSITY PRESS
1981

Library of Congress Cataloging in Publication Data
Main entry under title:

Change and the Muslim World

   (Contemporary issues in the Middle East)
   "Based on presentations . . . at a two-day
conference 'The World of Islam from Morocco to
Indonesia,' held in Washington, D.C., in June 1980,
and supplemented by additional material prepared or
solicited by the editors"—Pref.
   Bibliography: p.
   Includes index.
   1. Islam—20th century—Congresses. 2. Islamic
countries—Congresses. I. Stoddard, Philip.
II. Cuthell, David C. III. Sullivan, Margaret W.
IV. Series.
BP60.C42   909'.097671   81-18267
ISBN 0-8156-2251-1   AACR2

1924015

Contents

Contributors

WALTER K. ANDERSEN is research analyst for India and Indian Ocean affairs at the U.S. Department of State and adjunct faculty member in the School of Government at The American University, Washington, D.C. Recipient of a Ph.D. from the University of Chicago, he has written extensively on Indian domestic politics and foreign policy. He has taught at St. John's College and The College of Wooster and managed an undergraduate language training program in India for the Great Lakes Colleges Association.

ALEXANDRE BENNIGSEN is directeur d'études, École des Hautes Études, University of Paris. Since 1971, he has also served as visiting professor, department of history, University of Chicago. A native of St. Petersburg, Russia, he writes frequently on Muslims in the Soviet Union and on post-Mongol Eastern Europe in the fifteenth and sixteenth centuries.

PETER J. BERTOCCI teaches anthropology and South Asian civilization at Oakland University, Rochester, Michigan. He is a graduate of the Johns

Hopkins University School of Advanced International Studies and received a Ph.D. from Michigan State University. He has specialized in research on problems of rural political economy in Bangladesh.

WILLEM BIJLEFELD is director of the Center for the Study of Islam, Hartford Seminary Foundation, and editor of the journal *Muslim World*. He received his Doctorate in Theology from the University of Groningen, the Netherlands, and a Doctorate of Theology *cum laude* from the University of Utrecht. He lived in Nigeria serving as advisor to the Islam in Africa project and as assistant professor in the department of religious studies and the department of Arabic and Islamic studies at the University of Nigeria at Ibadan. Born in Indonesia, he has traveled extensively in South Asia, the Middle East, and Africa, lecturing at both Muslim and Christian universities and colleges.

DAVID C. CUTHELL is a retired Foreign Service Officer with overseas service in Australia, the Philippines, Greece, and eight years in Turkey. He also served several tours in Washington, including one as director of the Department of State office handling U.S. relations with the southwest Pacific during the period of Indonesia's confrontation with Malaysia and the abortive communist coup in Indonesia in 1965. A graduate of Yale, while in the foreign service Cuthell did graduate work at the Johns Hopkins University School of Advanced International Studies in Islamic history, religion, and theory.

NAFISSA AHMED EL AMIN is a member of the Politburo of the Sudanese Socialist Union, responsible for women's, youth, and parent and teachers' organizations. A founder of the Sudanese Women's Union and its current president, she has served as Deputy Minister of Youth, Sport, and Social Affairs and has been a member of three successive National Assemblies.

DONALD K. EMMERSON is associate professor of political science at the University of Wisconsin, Madison. His interest in Islam dates from Princeton undergraduate fieldwork on the Ahmadiyya movement in Nigeria. As a graduate student from Yale in the late 1960s he studied political culture in Indonesia, and returned in the mid-70s to study cultural politics. Islam was a major focus on both occasions, resulting in a book, *Indonesia's Elite*.

ELIZABETH W. FERNEA teaches at the Center for Middle Eastern Studies and the Department of English, University of Texas at Austin. Her books include *Guests of the Sheik* and *A Street in Marrakech*, as well as *Middle Eastern Muslim Women Speak* of which she is co-editor and translator.

TALAT SAIT HALMAN is Ambassador for Cultural Affairs, Permanent Mission of Turkey to the United Nations. He served as his country's Minister of Culture in 1971, and has taught at Princeton, Columbia, and New York universities. In addition to nearly twenty books in English and Turkish, he has published many articles on Turkey in the United States. He was also a columnist for two major Istanbul dailies, *Milliyet* and *Aksam*.

MUHAMMAD KAMAL BIN HASSAN is head of the Islamic studies program, National University of Malaysia. He was educated at the University of Malaysia and at Columbia University, where he earned Masters and Ph.D. degrees. He was previously head of the department of theology and philosophy at the National University of Malaysia. His writings have addressed the questions of education and Islam. Among them are *Developmental Significance of Islamic Education*.

SULAYMAN S. NYANG is associate professor of government and public administration at Howard University. Born in the Gambia, he holds M.A. and Ph.D. degrees from the University of Virginia. He also taught at that university and served as acting director of Howard University's African studies and research program. He served as deputy head of mission and head of chancery, Gambia Embassy, Jeddah, Saudi Arabia. Among his many publications are *Seminar Papers on African Studies* and the forthcoming works *Studies on Gambian Politics* and *Islam, Christianity, and African Identity*.

MALCOLM C. PECK is director of programs, The Middle East Institute. He holds degrees from Harvard University in Middle East studies, and a Ph.D. from the Fletcher School of Law and Diplomacy, Tufts University. He has taught at the University of Tennessee, Chattanooga, and was a post-doctoral research fellow at the Harvard University Center for Middle Eastern Studies. Author of numerous articles, he is currently preparing a book on the United Arab Emirates. He was a coordinator of the conference from which this volume is drawn.

BARBARA L. K. PILLSBURY is an associate professor at San Diego State University, currently on leave to the U.S. Agency for International Development. A social anthropologist, she has conducted research on Islam and Muslims in China for ten years. She lived among Chinese Muslims on Taiwan for three years in the early 1970s and in 1978 visited Muslims in the People's Republic of China. She holds a Ph.D. from Columbia University and has just completed a book, *Mosque and Pagoda: The Muslim Chinese*.

FAZLUR RAHMAN is professor of Islamic thought at the University of Chicago. He holds an M.A. from Punjab University in Lahore and a Ph.D. from Oxford University. He was a lecturer at the University of Durham, then associate professor of Islamic studies at the Institute of Islamic Studies, McGill University, and joined the Central Institute of Islamic Research of the Government of Pakistan, serving as director, 1962-68. The most recent of his many books is *Islam*.

ROUHOLLAH K. RAMAZANI is chairman and Edward R. Stettinius professor, Woodrow Wilson department of government and foreign affairs, University of Virginia. He was formerly vice president of the American Institute of Iranian Studies and visiting Aga Khan professor of Islamic studies, American University of Beirut, and visiting professor at Cambridge University and the Johns Hopkins University School of Advanced International Studies. The most recent of his many books is *The Persian Gulf and the Strait of Hormuz*.

MOWAHID H. SHAH, of Lahore, Pakistan, is a member of the District of Columbia Bar, currently associated with Reynolds, Mundy and Gibson. He received his LL.B. from Punjab University and an LL.M. in international law from George Washington University. He lectures and writes on matters of international interest. A *Worldview* article, "The Death of Bhutto and the Future of Pakistan," was widely translated in Pakistan.

MARGARET W. SULLIVAN is assistant director of the Washington Center of The Asia Society and was a conference coordinator for the session from which this manuscript derived. Over the past twenty-five years, she has lived and worked in five countries with majority or substantial minority Muslim populations: Malaysia, Indonesia, the southern Philippines, northern Nigeria, and Sierra Leone. She was a lecturer in English at the arts faculty of the University of Indonesia, and she conducted major research on traditional skills and village life in Sierra Leone. A graduate of American University, she consults as a senior intercultural communications specialist for the Business Council for International Understanding Institute.

PHILIP H. STODDARD has been involved in Middle East and Islamic affairs for three decades as student, teacher, and government specialist. Currently a deputy assistant secretary in the U.S. Department of State's Bureau of Intelligence and Research, he is a graduate of the University of Illinois and holds advanced degrees from Princeton University. A former Marine, he has taught in New York's state university system and at George Washington and American Universities in Washington, D.C., in addition to several years of research in Turkey and Egypt and frequent visits to the Middle East and South Asia.

JOHN WATERBURY is associate professor of politics and international affairs, Woodrow Wilson School for Public and International Affairs, Princeton University. He received a Ph.D. in political science from Columbia University. He has lived in the Middle East, and has written frequently on Moroccan and Egyptian politics. Author of *Hydropolitics of the Nile Valley*, he is currently at work on a book on the political economy of contemporary Egypt.

Preface

$\mathcal{T}$HIS VOLUME IS BASED ON PRESENTATIONS by more than a dozen experts, Muslim and non-Muslim, Americans and non-Americans, at a two-day conference, "The World of Islam from Morocco to Indonesia," held in Washington, D.C., in June 1980, and supplemented by additional material prepared or solicited by the editors. Sponsored jointly by the Washington Center of The Asia Society, the Middle East Institute, the National Committee to Honor the Fourteenth Centennial of Islam, and The John Hopkins University School of Advanced International Studies, the conference was made possible in part by grants from the National Endowment for the Humanities and the U.S. International Communication Agency.

The contributors to this book reflect a broad spectrum of views, both geographically and conceptually. Geographically, their essays cover the world of Islam from Africa, through the Middle East, and across Asia. Conceptually, the essays focus on the unifying values, the activism, and the major issues the Islamic world faces in the 1980s, in the light of its geographic breadth and cultural diversity.

The organizational principles behind the various essays are geographic, cultural, and national plurality, on the one hand, and transcending issues, on the other. Foremost among these issues is the impact of the process of modernization on Islamic societies, with emphasis on politics, education, and family life across the Muslim world and among Muslim communities in primarily non-Muslim countries. The rapid, yet differential, rates of change in most Muslim countries underline the timeliness of this approach.

Unlike most works on Islam, this volume presents contributors whose views cover a wide range of differing assumptions and perceptions. The essays address cogently and concisely the interaction between politics and religion and the difficult accommodations that Muslim countries and communities are seeking to the confrontation of development and tradition. Like the world of Islam itself, the contributors to this volume speak with both a single voice and many voices and present a mosaic of views. The editors have retained as much as possible of the style of the individual essays so that our contributors can speak for themselves and so that the diversity that permeates the Muslim community can shine forth. Though by no means are all Muslim countries and communities represented in this book, it contains a fair sample of the thinking about Islam today by Muslims and non-Muslims.

This book could not have come into being without a great deal of help and encouragement from many sources. The conference from which it grew brought together over four hundred people from many walks of life who were convinced that their need to explore Islam was worth staying inside on two of the most perfect June days 1980 produced. Their insightful questions and the excitement the conference engendered was added impetus to take a remarkable collection of papers and turn them into printed form. In addition to the contributors to this volume, special acknowledgment must be made of the others who participated in the conference panels and whose ideas are deeply embodied in the entire work: Macaparton Yahya Abbas, Jr., Imam Khalil Abdel Alim, John Duke Anthony, Abubaker Bagader, Lucius Battle, Dean Brown, Sevinc Carlson, William Crawford, Asad Hussain, Robert B. Oxnam, Abdurrachman Wahid, and R. Bayly Winder. George Packard, Dean of the Johns Hopkins University School of Advanced International Studies, not only participated in a panel but made it possible for the conference to take place at SAIS.

The glossary and the annotated bibliography of this volume were originally prepared as part of the briefing material for the conference. They are printed here with permission of The National Committee to Honor the Fourteenth Centennial of Islam which distributes them as part of a larger packet of basic information on Islam. Many individuals helped in its preparation and commented on its accuracy: Dr. Naomi F. Collins, Malcolm Peck and Margaret Sullivan edited; Dr. Mohammed Abdul-Rauf, Aisha and Faard Gouverneur, Laraine Carter and Cynthia Finlayson were particularly helpful in their comments. Liz Nichols and Carol Brown have put in endless hours of typing.

Finally, we must acknowledge with thanks the generous support of the Exxon Corporation and Texaco Inc.

Washington, D.C.   PHS
July 1981   DCC
                                                                              MWS

Change and the Muslim World

OF ISLAM...

U.S.S.R. 16%

Mongolia 4%

People's Republic of China 3%

Afghanistan 99%

Pakistan 97%

Nepal 5%

Arab Emirates 96%

Bangladesh 83%

India 11%

Burma 4%

Oman 100%
(den) 100%

Thailand 4%

Philippines 4%

100%

Sri Lanka 6%

Malaysia
mainland 53%
Sabah 38%
Sarawak 23%
Singapore 15%

Brunei 60%

Maldives 100%

Indonesia 90%

Fiji 8%

r 7%

auritius 16%

Sources:
*U.S. State Department
Fact Book, 1979.
The Muslim Peoples. A
World Ethnographic
Survey, Richard W.
Weekes, 1978.
U.S. State Department
Country Offices.
The Embassy of Nepal*

What Is Islam?

PROLOGUE

ISLAM IS AT ONCE A RELIGION AND A TOTAL WAY OF LIFE. Almost a fifth of the world's people—700 to 800 million in some sixty countries—are Muslims, embracing this faith first preached by the Prophet Muhammad fourteen centuries ago in the Arabian Peninsula. The world of Islam (*dar al-Islam*) stretches from the heartland of Saudi Arabia eastward through west Asia and the Indian subcontinent to Indonesia—the largest Muslim country—and the southern Philippines, northward into central Asia and southeastern Europe, and westward across north and sub-Saharan Africa and the Atlantic into South and North America.

This geographic spread contains people of many races and cultures, thus creating diversity among Muslims. They are unified by their common faith, Islam.

A FAITHFUL WAY OF LIFE: "GOD IS ONE"

What is it that Muslims share, be they Africans or Arabs, Asians or Americans? They share above all a belief in a single, all-powerful God, the same God worshipped by Jews and Christians. Their faith is summed up in the creed: "There is no god but God; Muhammad is the Messenger of God" (the *shahadah*).

Allah is the name of God in Arabic and in fact means "*the* God," to emphasize that "He is One and there is no other." Islam means "submission," connoting that submission to God brings health, peace, and justice. Islam also refers to the worldwide "nation" or community of all believers. These believers are Muslims (also spelled Moslems)—that is, "those who submit to the will of Allah."

Islam is not just a religion, if religion means only a system of belief and worship; rather, Islam is a total way of life. It proclaims faith and sets forth rituals. It also prescribes order for individuals and society in such areas as law, family relationships, matters of business, etiquette, dress, food, personal hygiene and much more. Islam is a complete, complex civilization in which, ideally, individuals, societies, and governments must all reflect the will of God. In essence, it is a system of rules or laws to be followed in which the sacred is not separated from the secular. The Western concept of such separation is alien to Islamic thought. As a faith structured by laws, Islam more closely parallels the legalistic Judaic system than the broadly stated principles of Christianity.

Part of the central message of Islam is:
• there is only one God
• all men are equal
• man achieves dignity through knowledge

Life on earth is believed to be a passage to a lasting and more worthy life. All people will be resurrected and rewarded according to their deeds.

THE KORAN: THE WORD OF GOD

The teachings of Islam are found in the Koran (*al-Quran*, or "recitation") which Muslims hold to be the immutable word of God and the unrivaled source of authority in almost all aspects of individual and group living. They believe it was revealed through the angel Gabriel in Arabic to the Prophet Muhammad (A.D. 570–632). Muhammad was commanded to recite the revelations he received from God. Muslims the world over, no matter what their tongues, memorize and recite the Koran in Arabic.

The Koran came to be supplemented by the traditions and sayings (*hadith*), anecdotes about what Muhammad said or did, as remembered by his Companions and passed down to suceeding generations as part of the sunnah, the "beaten path" for devout Muslims to follow. The sunnah recounts the deeds, sayings, and silent approval of the Prophet covering details of community life.

The Koran and the sunnah provide the framework for the *shariah*, Islam's body of law, In many, but not all, Islamic countries, the *shariah* still provides the legal basis for judgment and punishment. Although problems in dealing with non-Muslims and the colonial imposition of other legal systems have caused the *shariah* to be supplemented with Western legal codes in some countries, many Muslim nations have recently extended and reinforced the application of Islamic law.

THE FIVE PILLARS AND OTHER PRACTICES

Islam has five essential practices or "pillars of faith." These are:
- bearing witness (*shahadah*)
- praying (*salah*)
- giving alms (*zakah*)
- fasting (*sawm*)
- making the pilgrimage (*hajj*)

Daily prayers are performed by practicing Muslims either individually or, preferably, in a group. There are five daily prayer times—dawn, noon, afternoon, sunset, and night. When the time for prayer comes, in many countries Muslims stop whatever they are doing, ritually wash themselves, and pray. Facing a common shrine, the Kabah in Mecca, symbolizes unity of purpose for the millions of Muslims offering their prayers at the same time. Prayers said in mosques (the Muslim place of worship) have greater merit. While prayers are said daily, Friday is an Islamic day of communal prayer. These prayers are led by an *imam*. However, this function does not give him any special religious status. Similarly, the call to prayer, *azan*, is chanted by a man of the community, the *muezzin* who happens to have a particularly good voice, rather than someone who claims religious status. The call to prayer begins *Allahu Akbar*, "God is Great," a cry heard throughout the Muslim world.

Because of the uncompromising nature of Islamic monotheism, no images or pictures of any kind are permitted in the mosque. Islam preaches that all men are equal. Therefore, there are no pews or reserved places for dignitaries. The mosque is usually furnished with simple mats or with rugs. Worshipers form lines behind the *imam* as they arrive with no distinction of rank.

The belief in the equality of all men further means that Islam rejects the concept of *ordained* clergy. There are, nonetheless, religious leaders, many of whom exert power in the political as well as the strictly theological sphere, and who may be venerated by their followers. Since Islam includes all believers, there is no such thing as a separate "church."

In addition to the "five pillars," there are other practices commonly observed throughout the Islamic world. Muslims are forbidden to use intoxicating beverages or to consume pork, blood, or anything that might be harmful. In order to be eaten, animals must be ritually slaughtered and drained of blood. Similar dietary laws are found in Judaism.

There are no prescribed patterns of dress, except that women should cover their hair, arms, and legs, and men must cover the area from their navels to their knees. Customs in different Muslim societies reflect a range of interpretation. Women in some areas of the Muslim world are covered completely from head to toe, while in other places they dress demurely and some of them cover their heads with a scarf. In still others, women dress as they do in the West.

Many customs are currently under active discussion in the Muslim world, including the roles of women. The Koran states that God created all mankind from a male and a female, and as all are equal, none is better than another in His sight except through good deeds. Within Islam, women, like men, have moral and religious duties and are viewed as responsible. In the words of the Prophet, basic education is a right and also a duty for both men and women. Marriage and family are important. Sexual activities within marriage are meritorious; outside that bond, premarital or extramarital sex is a serious offense, punishable under the law of Islam. The degree to which men's and women's lives are separated, and women's lives are restricted, varies considerably in Muslim societies and is determined by custom and the way in which Islamic law is locally applied. The custom of keeping women in partial seclusion practiced in parts of the Muslim world seems oppressive to Westerners and to some modernist Muslims but is viewed by many other Muslims as being protective and respectful of women.

These and other unifying beliefs and practices shape and define Muslims. Theirs is at once a faith and a way of life centered on individual and communal submission to the will of the One God. Within this faith, what is the position of Muhammad?

MUHAMMAD IS GOD'S MESSENGER

Islam teaches that God revealed His existence to a number of prophets through the ages. They include Adam, Noah, Abraham, Moses, and Jesus. According to Muslims, however, God's final and complete revelation was given to Muhammad.

Muhammad was born in Mecca, in what is now Saudi Arabia, about A.D. 570. He was unsatisfied with the pagan religions of his people as well as with the prevailing social conditions, and contemplated religious and social questions. As a caravan merchant and subsequent leader of the embryonic Meccan community, Muhammad came into contact with Jews, Christians, and other monotheists who worshipped a single God.

During one of his frequent meditations alone in the desert hills near Mecca in the lunar month of Ramadan in A.D. 610 Muhammad heard revelations from the angel Gabriel and began to receive the Koran. This process of revelation continued for some twenty-three years. At God's commandment, the Prophet Muhammad began reciting God's word and preaching the message revealed to him. His wife Khadijah and some of his relatives and closest friends were the first believers. The ruling oligarchy in Mecca fought bitterly to stamp out this movement. During this period, tradition holds that Muhammad went on a night journey in which he was transported from Mecca to the site of The Dome of the Rock in Jerusalem and from there ascended to heaven for a preview of the afterlife. (According to biblical tradition, the Dome of the Rock is the site on which Abraham was prepared to sacrifice his son, and is revered by Jews, Christians, and Muslims. Next to it has been built the *Aqsa Mosque*, one of Islam's most sacred places of worship.)

In 622, after continued persecution, Muhammad and his followers left Mecca and took refuge in Yathrib, which came to be known as *al Madina*, "the City." This emigration (*hijrah*) marks the year one of the Islamic calendar. A.H., used in denoting years in this calendar, stands for Anno Hegirae, "in the year of the emigration," in the same way A.D. stands for Anno Domini, "in the year of Our Lord."

In Medina, Muhammad became the ruler of the community as well as its religious teacher. Both the Koran and the examples of the Prophet governed daily life and gave the community its laws. Muhammad gathered more and more followers and, eight years later, returned to Mecca victorious. There he smashed the idols in and around the temple called the Kabah, but saved its black stone reputedly given earlier in history by the angel Gabriel to Abraham. The Grand Mosque erected around the Kabah is the most holy place in Islam and marks the direction in which Muslims pray. Mecca, Medina and Jerusalem are Islam's holiest cities because of their connections with Muhammad's life and because of the mosques that have been built to commemorate these events. Before he died in A.D. 632 Muhammad was able to break down many tribal loyalties and unify his followers who came from other groups.

In Islam, Muhammad is honored as God's final Prophet. He did not create but received the Koran. Muslims do not worship Muhammad, only

Allah. It is incorrect, consequently, to call Muslims—those who submit to the will of God—Muhammadans.

"PEOPLE OF THE BOOK"

Muhammad is viewed by Muslims as the last in a succession of prophets who preached parts of the same message. Earlier sacred writings, the Torah, the Psalms, and the Gospel of Jesus, are often mentioned in the Koran. In contrast to pagans, who worshipped idols and believed in many gods, Jews and Christians are called "people of the book," and are given special protection under Muslim law. The Koran states: "Be courteous when you argue with People of the Book, except with those of them who do evil. Say 'we believe in that which is revealed to us and that which was revealed to you. Our God and your God is One. To Him we surrender ourselves.'"

Jesus is granted particular respect by Muslims. However, because of their belief in the oneness of God, they reject the Christian concept of the Trinity. Respecting "people of the book" underlines the common heritage Muslims believe that they share with Christians and Jews.

SUNNIS, SHIAHS, AND SUFIS

When Muhammad died, a dispute arose over leadership of the Muslim community, which was also the first Islamic state. One faction, the sunnis (derived from the Arabic word for "custom" or "use"), felt that the Caliph (*khalifah*, Arabic for "successor") should be chosen, as Arab chiefs customarily were, by election. Therefore they supported the succession of the first four, or "rightly guided," Caliphs, who had been Muhammad's Companions.

The other group thought that Muhammad chose his cousin, son-in-law and the fourth caliph, Ali as his immediate heir, and that succession should be through his bloodline. In A.D. 680 one of Ali's sons, Hussein, led a band of rebels against the ruling Caliph and they were massacred. Hussein's martyrdom began the shiah (sometimes called shiite) movement, whose name comes from a word meaning "partisans of Ali."

The shiah and the sunni are the two major branches of Muslims, with the sunni comprising about 85 percent of the total. The differences between these two major sects are not so much in belief or law, which are fundamentally the same for both, as in practice and political theory. The shiah (Shiism is the state religion in Iran and shii form a majority in Iraq) have developed a hierarchical religious leadership. Both the shiah and sunni are further divided among themselves in theology, practice, and political structure of government.

Cutting across these sects is sufism. Sufism is a mystical strain of Islam which reflects the need felt by many Muslims to realize in their personal experience the living presence of God.

Sufism emphasizes the cultivation of individual piety through private devotion, public ritual, and practical charity. It began as an ascetic movement in the early centuries of Islam and evolved into a complex theory of mystical discipline and then into a highly developed theosophy. The twelfth and thirteenth centuries saw the beginning of the institution—the *tariqah*, variously translated as dervish order, fraternity, or brotherhood (or more accurately as the sufi path that leads one to communication with God)—that thereafter dominated the sufi movement and that lay behind its mass appeal. The brotherhoods, of which there have been a great number, have emphasized shared ritual, discipline, and the communal life.

Taken collectively, sufi orders, which have colored much of the religious life of later Islam, have tended to have two common characteristics: they have often been at odds with the legalists of the Islamic establishment, and they have been the great missionaries of Islam. Tough and resilient under pressure, the brotherhoods have made progress at the popular level in place of more intellectual orthodoxy.

As a mass movement, sufism swept rapidly through the entire Muslim world and, through its close association with popular religion, played an important role in the diffusion of Islam in such diverse areas as northwest Africa, black Africa, Central Asia, the USSR (where Islam's survival under Soviet pressure owes much to illegal sufi orders), and India.

THE SPREAD OF ISLAM

Perhaps no single historical event between the fall of Rome and the European voyages of discovery was more significant than the rise of Islam. Islam provided a focus for political order and intellectual growth affecting the entire world, not just those people who embraced it.

By conversion, commerce, and conquest, the new faith spread quickly in all directions soon after its founding. During a period of world chaos and the breakdown of existing empires, people saw Islam as a comprehensive faith and political/legal system which provided order and justice.

To describe the expansion in general terms, however, Islam soon brought North Africa under its sway. In the Middle East, from modern Iraq to the Atlantic, most of the converts became Arabized, adopting the Arabic language and assimilating Islamic culture. Elsewhere conversion did not bring Arabization. (Today only fifteen to twenty percent of all Muslims are Arabs). Within a century, Islam had spread to northern Spain in the West and India in the East.

Although this initial expansion was halted in France in A.D. 732, Sicily and parts of Europe were later conquered. The Ottoman Turks later added most of previously Christian southeastern Europe to the domain of Islam. In a different direction, Islam crossed the Sahara into the kingdoms of black Africa. Arab Muslims and non-Arab converts carried Islam beyond India into central Asia and to what are now Malaysia, Indonesia, and a part of the southern Philippines.

The rise of Islam not only brought empires into being, it also fostered the flowering of civilizations and the development of centers of learning. A melding of new thought with ancient, of ideas from East and West took place, producing great contributions in medicine, mathematics, physics, astronomy, geography, architecture, art, language, literature, and history. Eventually crucial ideas and concepts were transmitted, either directly or indirectly, from Islamic centers to medieval Christian Europe. Much ancient Greek learning was passed on. Such basic mathematical concepts as Arabic numerals, algebra, and the idea of zero were refined and later conveyed into European thought. Sophisticated instruments which were to make possible the European voyages of discovery were developed, among them the astrolabe, the quadrant, and improved navigational maps.

From the seventh to the eleventh centuries, the community of Muslims was economically and militarily more powerful than Christian Europe, rivaling Chinese civilization in its achievements. However, Islam's success in spreading rapidly over such an expanse of territories and peoples led to political fragmentation. It was this which in the twelfth and thirteenth centuries made possible the Christian Crusades, events still remembered by Muslim Arabs as Western aggression. While in the fifteenth and sixteenth centuries the Ottomans reimposed some political unity, the original dynamism of Islamic civilization slowed and an enduring equilibrium of forces in many Islamic societies was struck.

In the meantime, Europe discovered new well-springs of vitality, partly fed from Islamic sources. The Renaissance in the fourteenth to seventeenth centuries led to the creation of powerful secular institutions, in particular the nation-state. The Protestant Reformation, with its emphasis on the importance and potential of the individual, complemented the Renaissance. Advancements in science and the Industrial Revolution generated new methods of organization and of the generation of power. Europe was therefore able to dominate large portions of the rest of the world, including much of the Muslim world. The New World grew out of the European voyages of discovery, and the Industrial Revolution spawned both capitalist and communist theory, which have defined the systems of the present superpowers.

Both the earlier period of Muslim dominance and the later reversal of historical fortunes have created stereotypes and misperceptions of Islam in the non-Muslim world. These are reinforced by the lack of contact between most Westerners and Muslims. Hence Islam—in many ways closely related to Western civilization—is often seen as hostile, dangerous, or incomprehensible. Complex forces are sweeping Islam that affect not only Muslims but also the entire world. Understanding these forces is further complicated by misperceptions.

THE PRESENT: MATERIAL PROGRESS AND SPIRITUAL VALUES

In our own time, the impact of industrial development, technology, urbanization, and secular values has had far-reaching consequences. Around the world, rapid change has disrupted social patterns and cultural traditions which served as reference points for centuries. Muslims, no less than others, are reacting. Along with the flood of Western technology have come new, sometimes unwelcome ideas concerning individualism, materialism, sexuality, family, and politics. To some, these ideas seem to threaten basic Islamic values. Furthermore, the outlook of most Muslims is strongly colored by a very recent emergence from a long period of foreign domination. There is also an awareness of the clearly visible economic disparities between industrialized and developing nations and, within societies, between classes.

Concerned Muslims across Asia and Africa are actively exploring many routes to find the balance between modernization and tradition. This reflects a sense among Muslims that Islamic principles may offer them more appropriate solutions to their national problems than those offered by either capitalism or communism. Therefore they call for a reinjection of basic Islamic values into the lives of the individual and society. Among the varied responses advocated by a vocal minority has been a resurgent call for Islamic revival. This response is closely related to similar outpourings around the world.

Just as Muslims are culturally diverse, so too there is no single "Islamic" politics or economics. What unites concerned Muslims is determination to strengthen and preserve their heritage. Islam is at once a religion and a way of life.

1

Themes and Variations

Philip H. Stoddard

THE WORLD OF ISLAM, after fourteen centuries of development, has forced itself on the American consciousness only recently. Before the sudden rise in the price of oil in late 1973 and 1974, Islam was largely unknown to most of the West. Since 1974, however, many Americans and other Westerners have found themselves deeply troubled by developments in the Islamic world. They sense what Edward Said has called in *Harper's* an "unprecedented potential for loss and disruption" at the hands of Muslims and worry about their own lack of knowledge of what Islam is and is not. Yet they seem convinced, and rightly so, that Muslims and Americans increasingly will be involved with one another.

THE MEDIA

Americans were deluged by waves of commentary about Islam during the 444 days our fellow citizens were held hostage in Tehran. We have been bombarded with provocative terms like the "Islamic explosion," the "historic

The views expressed here are Dr. Stoddard's own and not necessarily those of the U.S. Department of State.

whirlwind" of militant Islam, Islam the "ideology of martyrdom," the "crescent of crisis," and the "arc of instability." More recently, ferment and frustration, revival and resurgence, complexity and diversity have crept into the lexicon of contemporary commentary about Islam.

The media tend to see Islam as an anti-American monolith and Islam's attitude toward us as the yardstick by which to measure its validity. Descriptions of trends in the Islamic world generally have ignored the diversity of Muslim peoples and the debate on fundamental issues that permeates the Islamic world.

CONSTANCY AND CHANGE

Islam, after all, has been and will remain a world religion. The Muslim community has witnessed phenomenal growth over the centuries, through what Fazlur Rahman calls in his book, *Islam*, its "inner intensity of life." As a religious and political complex, Islam has retained the loyalty of followers in the Middle East, North Africa, Central Asia, the Indian sub-continent, Malaysia, and Indonesia; and in sub-Saharan Africa and elsewhere it apparently continues to expand. Islam has survived and prospered because of its symbiotic relationship with its adherents: Islam guides and sustains a variety of key institutions, especially the community and family, that in turn nourish Islam.

Islam is an active force in the lives of its adherents. It is neither a way of life manipulated by unshaven zealots in turbans nor an unresponsive religious system divorced from the lives of the faithful. Indeed, throughout its long history, Islam has never been unchanging. It has made innumerable adjustments and compromises as a result of its internal processes of questioning and reform, and it has acquired a richness and depth of experience that has enabled it to meet challenges creatively.

Islam, as it enters its fifteenth century, is undergoing an extended period of rapid and far-reaching changes. These changes—social, political, economic, and cultural—are unsettling and inevitable. They result in part from the impact of new ideas and technologies, and the need to react to them, and in part from the practical problems raised by national independence and sovereignty, concepts new to most Muslim societies. Nevertheless, it is wrong and misleading to view the ferment in the Islamic world as stemming solely from Islam's response to external challenges. As Bernard Lewis has noted in *The New York Times Magazine*, Islam is not "merely passive and reactive."

THE CHALLENGE

A basic problem for Islamic states today seems to be to determine, in Dr. Rahman's words, "what Islam may modify and what it may reject." Responding to this challenge is at the core of much of the ferment in the Muslim world. Muslims now face what many of them see as an internal struggle, and they are trying to understand the dynamic forces at work in their varied environments.

The turbulence in the Muslim world makes even more important our need to examine carefully the processes of reaction and adjustment to external and internal stimuli that have been so greatly influenced by religion, tradition, and, in many cases, the colonial experience. The contributors to this book try in their different ways to disentangle the real from the unreal and thus help us reject the stereotypes and misinformation that pervade much of the commentary on the Muslim world. In this way we can identify and understand the trends that will have a significant impact on us all in coming years.

STEREOTYPES AND MISPERCEPTIONS

For most of us, Islam, despite its monotheism, seems to rest on an alien conception. We tend to analyze and explain Islam in Western terms that sometimes portray Muslims as backward peoples, homogeneous (usually Arab) and unchanging, whose behavior follows unfamiliar patterns. We often continue the stereotype in our application to Islam of such concepts as "modernization" and "reform" which do not conform very well with Islam's history and tradition. Most Westerners seem uneasy when contemplating a religious system that traditionally views state and faith as one, and in which religious belief, in theory, governs both conduct and politics.

Certainly Islam is different from other religions, and many Muslims regard cause and effect and other concepts that scientifically educated persons take for granted from a different vantage point than we like to think we do since, for them, God is the ultimate cause. But American views swing widely between regarding Muslims as quietistic fatalists, on one hand, and aggressive xenophobes, on the other. Moreover, it is difficult to try to determine which attitudes and customs derive from Islam and which are the result of culture, history, and the human condition.

It is illuminating to remember that Muslim states are "Third World" states. Mostly poor, despite the few very wealthy oil exporters, they share many problems with and face the same challenges as other poor states whose poverty and often painful histories produce strong feelings of insecurity. Yet, as we see in the essays in this book, there are innumerable variations among Muslims—even within a particular Muslim country—often derived from social status, level of education, and extent of exposure to the outside world.

Against this backdrop, we should examine our fondness for unidimensional interpretations of complex processes and events. We should recall, when examining our perceptions of Islam, that stereotypes, especially those of nations and large populations, by definition, are gross exaggerations. As Bayly Winder recently pointed out in *The New York Times*, the West tends "to underestimate and denigrate the technological and professional capabilities" of peoples of the Third World, whether they apply to operating the Suez Canal or oil refineries in Iran. Despite major cultural differences, he notes, all peoples can learn to meet high standards of dedication and professionalism.

Harvey Cox has written eloquently in *The Atlantic* of our inability to "find much to admire in Islam" and of our tendency to think of Islam in images that interfere with our ability to understand Islam. We might ask ourselves why so many of us feel unsympathetic toward a faith with 800 million adherents. Perhaps it is the historical sense of threat or the many apparent similarities among Judaism, Christianity, and Islam that make Islam, despite its rich core of tradition, seem mostly derivative.

For these reasons, a multidisciplinary approach to Islam that stresses both differentiation and uniformity is required. This volume, the reader will note, does not deal with Islamic economics. That subject is worthy of separate study.

COMMON THEMES

Generalizations about the world of Islam are perilous, as our contributors make clear in their presentations. There is no single "Muslim world." Instead there are sovereign nation-states, some of which are less Islamic than others.

Variations in the process of change in each Muslim state and a great diversity of institutions, cultures, and historical experience recur in the reactions and adjustments of Muslim states and communities to the challenges they face. Such themes as unity, revival, and resilience appear and reappear in the essays in this book. Some of these themes, not surprisingly, receive more attention than others; we tend to focus on new trends and especially on those topics, such as the Islamic revival, that have received most of the attention in Western and Muslim commentary.

THE UNITY OF THE MANY "WORLDS" OF ISLAM

There is a sense of identification derived from a shared religious commitment to Islam as a complete and unified way of life, even in such diverse countries as Saudi Arabia and Indonesia, and among the large Muslim communities in China and India. Muslims share a set of beliefs, a revealed scripture, a system of worship, a strong sense of belonging to a community of believers, and an integrated system of law—the *shariah*—that is both secular and religious and that traditionally recognizes no dichotomy between the religious and the secular.

REVIVAL AND RESURGENCE

The increasing activism of Muslims has received considerable attention, especially since the Iranian revolution, among both Western and Muslim commentators on contemporary Islam, and many of the sixteen essays in this volume refer to it frequently. We should remember, however, that Islamic revival movements did not begin with the Iranian revolution. The Wahhabi revival in what is now Saudi Arabia, as Malcolm Peck observes in his essay, began in the eighteenth century, and the Muslim Brotherhood was founded in the 1920s. Yet the popular appeal of these movements was relatively limited geographically.

The manifestations of this phenomenon include ferment, restiveness, a hunger for an Islamic renaissance to deal with the breakdown of traditional patterns, and new dichotomies between "modernists" and "traditionalists." These cleavages become even wider as the overarching concepts of unity and community come under pressure from growing literacy, industrialization, urbanization, and the emergence of a technologically trained middle class, as well as changing sex roles, as Elizabeth W. Fernea points out in her perceptive essay on family life.

The ferment encompasses both a rejection of blind imitation of the West and a resentment of—even hostility toward—what is seen as the West's arrogance, ethnocentrism, and repression. It is often accompanied by tensions associated with the uneven distribution of the perceived benefits of the process of modernization, by a rebellion against secular politics, and by a resentment of modernization's assault on traditional value systems.

Reactions to these challenges vary widely. In some cases, Muslim governments have tried to highlight the role of Islam in national life and to enforce religious precepts from the top down—for example, prohibitions on alcohol and dancing, rules for governing clothing for women, and Islamic constitutions—as part of a turning back to Islam to create a sense of national unity and to find symbols of legitimacy, just as opposition groups use Islamic symbols to organize dissent. Other governments are seeking to preserve and develop their countries in accord with their conception of a good Islamic state, such as Saudi Arabia, which exemplifies the interplay of conservative Islam and politics.

In Iran, for example, as Rouhollah K. Ramazani observes in his essay, the reaction has been stern and harsh. In the spring of 1980 the regime of the clerics and their supporters launched, in the name of Islamic purity, a "cultural revolution." It rejected a broad definition of Islam as encompassing internationalism, cosmopolitanism, and humanitarianism in favor of a narrow view of Iran's culture and Islamic heritage. This clerical perspective was justified in terms of requirements for the struggle against the "idolatrous order" that was perceived as blocking the realization of a divinely based community.

On the other hand, the reaction may be flexible but impatient, as in the Sudan. Nafissa Ahmed el Amin highlights a restless search for identity and for a pattern of social change that can reconcile both spiritual development and material welfare through a process of adaptation and assimilation.

Further, in a search for Islamic roots, the reaction may hark back to a "golden age." This phenomenon seems especially prevalent among Muslims whose mobility is blocked or whose precarious existence is threatened by unfamiliar, and therefore even sinister, forces. At the same time, there is a perception among many Muslims that answers drawn from the past cannot cope with the complexities of the modern world and that the structure of establishment Islam cannot contain the anger of people who have been uprooted from their traditional milieu.

There are innumerable explanations of this unrest in the many Islamic "worlds." In part, it seems to stem from a growing disillusionment with various aspects of the processes of modernization and development, particularly the expectations of sharply improved economic conditions that cannot be fulfilled. Thus, conspicuous consumption, maldistribution of wealth, and corruption, and the popular association of these phenomena with the governments of some Muslim states, have bred resentment and have added to disillusionment.

There also seems to be a perception among many Muslims that, over the past century, their efforts to be taken seriously and to shape their own destinies have failed. The choice for many seems to have been one of either participating in the outside world, with all its risks, or turning inward and becoming less "modern."

Many Muslims ask why they seem to be falling behind in their quest for relevance, even after colonialism, in its direct forms, has faded away. They perceive that the fruits of liberation sometimes have turned sour, and that events occurring outside Islam are threatening to Islam and to Muslim communities. If imitation of the patterns that led to the "success" of the West has not worked, is it possible that a leadership role can be regained by anything other than a return to Islamic virtues and principles? Socialism and capitalism are perceived as having failed, massive arms purchases and large armies have not produced the anticipated strength, and economic development, which accentuates the assault on tradition, has not been a panacea.

As a result, there seems to be a sense of frustration, even betrayal, especially among the young, over the failure of social systems and governments to keep their promises for a better life in the broadest sense. The governments themselves, many of which assumed power with high hopes and broad popular support, are regarded in some cases as the corrupt handmaidens of the enemies of Islam.

These concerns have led to a series of informational publications and conferences by Muslims in many parts of the Islamic world. Permeating these articles, books, and speeches is an emphasis on recommitment to Islamic values of simplicity and adherence to tradition and first principles. (This desire for simplicity when confronted by challenges, of course, is not unique to Islam.) In this way, it is hoped, the tide of extraneous and alien ideologies, Westernization, and secularism (epitomized by the dethronement of the *shariah* in many Muslim states) can be reversed. By a great struggle to cleanse the original Islamic teachings of the accretions of later eras and to reinforce Islamic norms, Islamic society may be regenerated and made strong once again.

In all of this ferment is a large element of negativism and looking back. There is a heavy emotional emphasis on resurgence from a period of decadence and decline and on a return to the perceived purity of the earliest Islamic centuries. But the ferment encompasses more than a hankering for the past. It also manifests the enthusiasm inherent in setting off on a bold, new enterprise in which imported technology and industrialization will be used along with piety to confront internal pressures and to meet aspirations for employment, a rising standard of living, and a new sense of achievement. The result of this effort, many Muslims believe, will be a rebirth of confidence and a strengthening of Islam as a shaper of consensus, a protection against hostile ideologies, and the source of a renewed sense of identity and of what Professor Dekmejian has called an "escape from alienation."

The relationship between confidence and revival, on the one hand, and distress and frustration, on the other, is as complex and varied as the Muslim world itself. Like all great renaissance movements it combines pride, fear of failure, and sociopolitical trauma. It includes uneasy alliances between revolutionary programs and existing institutions, as well as ample criticism of present and past policies of governance and patterns of behavior.

We should note, however, that the ferment among Muslims and the current resurgence of Islamic fundamentalism, while widespread, do not appear to be the result of a universal Muslim revival movement nor do they proceed from a single center. Islamic fundamentalism is not dominated by a few key countries, and it lacks a unified leadership or a philosophy that transcends national boundaries. This is because of the extraordinary cultural diversity and the social and economic differences among the various Muslim states and communities. For these reasons, a replay of the Iranian revolution does not seem likely elsewhere.

On the issue of radicalism among Muslims, conventional wisdom holds that the younger generation in many Muslim countries will turn to radical and leftist ideologies if their political, economic, and social expectations are sufficiently frustrated. Yet the nature of the new strains of militant Islam found in North Africa, the Middle East, and Southeast Asia in the last few years casts doubt on this view. Many young Muslims undoubtedly will continue to seek meaning in their lives through radical secular channels, but Western forms of radicalism increasingly are being rejected in favor of indigenous variations based on religion or ethnicity.

Most important, behind these manifestations of ferment and resurgence lies the assumption on the part of many Muslims that militant, activist Islam will remain a permanent feature of many Islamic communities and nations. One feature of this activism is individual religious renewal, reflected in increased mosque attendance, keeping the fast during Ramadan and other less tangible manifestations of piety. This trend is particularly noticeable among the middle and upper classes in the Middle East and Southeast Asia.

It is also important to note that the growing inability of many societies to cope with the social disorientation caused by rapid and uneven change is not limited to the Muslim world, nor is the new fundamentalism limited to Muslims. Israel's militant Gush Emunin (Faith Bloc), Indian Hindus' Rashtriya Swayansevak Sangh (National Volunteer Association), and charismatic movements in the Roman Catholic and Episcopal churches are basically fundamentalist. Each group seems to be seeking meaning in life through a return to what it perceives as the fundamentals of religious belief.

But what distinguishes Islamic fundamentalism from fundamentalist movements elsewhere? The answer probably lies in Islamic cultural values and social norms that channel frustration with the changes associated with modernization along unique Islamic lines. In nearly every country of the Third World rapid change has created widespread psychological and social displacement without providing a new framework for personal, social, and political integration. In Muslim countries, religion exerts a particularly powerful appeal and conveys a sense of identity in a changing environment. It also promises a more just society in the future and is an especially potent force among the discontented and the left behind.

Of crucial importance in this regard is Islam's lack of distinction between the secular and the spiritual. Thus the secularization of Islamic society that accompanies modernization is widely perceived as threatening because it denies religious reinforcement of self-esteem. For this reason, rejection of secularization has become a major theme in Islamic revivalist movements.

RESILIENCE AND STEADFASTNESS

Despite the frustration among Muslims over their perceived situation, they are confident that Islam can make the necessary shifts, as it has in the past, through a process of continuous adaptation. Muslims share a conviction that Islamic values will be maintained even in the face of disruptive internal change and external pressure.

The essays in this volume reflect a strong feeling that Muslims view modernization and Islamic values as compatible, though not without political and social tensions. Moreover, the essays convey a determination that Islam as a religious system and as a way of life will survive and flourish, even in the face of major challenges—political, social, and economic. To this end, many Muslims are stressing in politics and family life the principles of Islam that have served the community well for so long. Even as traditional patterns are reexamined and reinterpreted, as Elizabeth Fernea comments in her essay, the conviction remains that the family is the institution best suited to solving social problems and to providing the common bonds that are essential to see people through difficult times of social pressure, transition, and transformation.

In a fundamental sense, many Muslims are adapting to the new by emphasizing old values and patterns of living that have provided a strong sense of identity and purpose in the past.

VARIETY AND DIVERSITY

Even a cursory examination of the seventeen essays in this volume reveals the variety of the Muslim experience across the broad sweep of the Islamic world. In Bangladesh, an area no larger than Wisconsin, is the world's second largest

Muslim nation. Peter J. Bertocci's essay indicates a balance among three traditions: Islam, Bengali culture, and nationalism, and a commitment to Western forms of modernization in which economic planning is Westernized and the educational system is both Western and Islamic. In Malaysia, an effort to integrate Islam's emphasis on spirituality and morality into the social structure is an important dimension in building an economically advanced society and in warding off a crisis of values, Muhammad Kamal bin Hassan tells us in his contribution.

Turkey is a different case. The "dark horses" of Islam, as Talat Halman calls the Turks in his essay, chose a separate path for dealing with the interaction of the West and traditional Muslim culture. Nationalism and secularism prevailed, epitomized by Ataturk's emphasis on revolutionary transformation from a "theocracy" to a "secular" nation-state. Yet the integration process is not complete: traditionalist sentiment survives; Islam remains the faith and the source of spiritual satisfaction and has found limited expression in political action and in an upsurge of Muslim practices. This revival, however, has not converted Turkey into an Islamic state. For Turks, Islam is spiritually edifying but not politically unifying.

In Indonesia, the most populous Muslim nation, Islam is politically enfeebled but culturally vigorous and syncretic. Though Islam is on the defensive, the government feels obliged to respect the sensibilities of the Muslim community, even as each feels threatened by the other. Our contributor, Donald K. Emmerson, notes that Indonesia is an archipelagic nation whose colonial history and ecologically and ethnolinguistically fragmented setting have blocked purity of ideology and consistency of belief and behavior, and thus have made more difficult a creative adaptation to a changing world.

Ironically, as Alexandre Bennigsen observes, in the USSR, despite many decades of harsh treatment, neither czars nor commissars have been able to obliterate all traces of the Islamic way of life. Islam in the Soviet Union is resilient and is undergoing a resurgence among the young people as a means of maintaining their culture against Russian domination. The success of this effort stems in large part from the activism of the outlawed but deeply rooted sufi brotherhoods.

In Egypt, where the sense of identity is strong and society highly integrated, Islam has penetrated deeply and is both a cause of dissension and a source of unity. As John Waterbury tells us in his perceptive essay, the "religious right" is potentially the most powerful and best organized political force, but it seems unable, in present circumstances, to alter Egypt's course in any fundamental way. This weakness seems to derive primarily from two factors: the diffusion of religious authority and the religious right's lack of effective leaders; and Sadat's success, so far, in shrewdly balancing the various political actors against a complex backdrop of substantial foreign aid and economic growth and vulnerability.

It is obviously not possible in an introductory essay to do justice to the cultural diversity and religious unity of the world of Islam. Cultural pluralism is the norm, yet these patterns rest on a common foundation. Should this diversity of social, economic, and political conditions, national characteristics and differing historical conditions among Muslims, asks Willem Bijlefeld in our concluding essay, be called Islamic diversity? How much of the reaction to the challenges that Muslims face is traceable to Islam and how much can be understood in non-Islamic terms?

Perhaps, as Dr. Bijlefeld eloquently suggests, we should start, as we read these essays, with the proposition that, "whatever the diversity of cultures, of political situations, of backgrounds, and of historical experience, we all have one thing in common: 'our humanity.'" On that basis, there is much to learn from the contributors to this volume about what the rest of the world shares with Muslims.

2

Roots of Islamic Neo-Fundamentalism

Fazlur Rahman

THE MANIFESTATION OF CONTEMPORARY ISLAM commonly referred to as Islamic fundamentalism is a product of the interaction of long historical development in Islam with the hegemony of the West during the past century and a half. Fundamentalism must be seen in this double perspective and not interpreted merely as an Islamic reaction to the West in the light of newly gained political independence.

Within the Islamic world there are certain common responses to the phenomenon of Islamic revivalism, but these are accompanied by a variety of views and attitudes that cannot be fully explained by local factors. Among these, for example, are the differing forms of conservatism of official Saudi Arabian policy and of President Zia of Pakistan, and the radicalism of Libya's Qadhafi. Within the concept of Islamic fundamentalism, we have to recognize and explain differences over such basic issues as the legitimacy, in Islamic terms, of political democracy and of modern banking. So too must we explain the highly ambivalent attitudes toward the West. Current Muslim attitudes are of immediate and often grave importance to the West. Understanding their essence and variations requires knowledge of their history.

BACKGROUND

A study of the history of revival and reform in Islam shows that moral rather than theological factors have been in the foreground. I do not mean to say that there have been no theological differences in Islam; indeed, there have been. Particularly in the early period (seventh to tenth centuries), there was a proliferation of theological views that can be called loosely schools rather than sects, of most of which nothing remains but their names. What does seem to have been the case, however, is that revival and reform in Islam resulted from a moral impulse. Although this impulse sometimes found a theological formulation, this formulation was secondary. The Shiah "Imamology" is perhaps the only major example in Islam of a theological formulation that bears little relationship to its genuine and concrete moral impulse, the essence of which is a deep sense of outrage at injustice and tyranny. What has kept Shiism apart from Sunnism is not so much this righteous anger at injustice, but the centrality of passion, based on the violent death of the Prophet's grandson Hussein and the doctrine of "Imamology" that flowed from it.

As a consequence, reform has not consisted of the formal acceptance or rejection of theological propositions. Islamic dogma is minimal; it has been said that in Islam one does not find orthodoxy but orthopraxy (correct practice). This statement is correct, provided it does not deny the existence of beliefs that, although they are primarily moral rather than theological, are directly concerned with practical life. The central place is occupied by the question of free will and its efficacy. This question has far reaching consequences for the nature of reform and the way it proceeds. Reform is not concerned with readjustments or reformulations of dogma. When orthodoxy is generally felt to espouse beliefs and attitudes which are conducive to or condone laxity, degeneracy, over-formalism, and ritualism, pressures build up around the center. Although these pressures are castigated as heretical, they eventually produce a reformulation of orthodoxy. Reform, therefore, is more in the nature of moral revitalization than of substantive change.

EARLY REFORMS

The cases of reform at the hands of al-Ghazzali (1058–1111) and Ibn Taymiyah (1263–1328) illustrate the truth of this proposition. The legacies of Ibn Taymiyah and al-Ghazzali germinated in the eighteenth century; they blossomed into important activist reform movements on the one hand and reformist intellectual ideas on the other. Modern writers have rightly emphasized the importance of activist phenomena in eighteenth century Islam, but have not sufficiently appreciated the intellectual components of Islam in that century. It is true, however, that as the eighteenth century reformist impulse worked itself out through the nineteenth century in the African and Indian reform movements, ethico-social activism became more prominent. It would be a serious mistake, however, to underestimate the silent but enduring ethico-spiritual and intellectual leaven emanating from al-Ghazzali's tradition. I should clarify that I am using al-Ghazzali and Ibn Taymiyah to symbolize respectively the intellectualist and activist trends within the Muslim community. This point is especially important because although the world is now preoccupied with the contemporary Islamic situation, which is palpably activist, I hope to show that the survival of the Islamic world as Islamic is conditioned not only on activist ferment, but on patient and complex intellectual labor which must produce the necessary Islamic vision.

ISLAMIC POSITIVISM

One important factor that is common to both the activist and intellectual traditions as they developed into premodernist reform phenomena of the eighteenth and nineteenth centuries is the importance of the concept of "obedience to God," i.e., obedience to God for its own sake and not primarily to avoid hell or gain paradise. To be sure, belief in the day of final accounting and in the reality of reward and punishment are there, but the stress is on "carrying out God's command." This subtle but fundamental shift in emphasis and focus on conduct in this world, of which the thought of Ibn Khaldun (1332–1406) is a monumental example, may be called "Islamic positivism." That Islam has been, from its genesis, not an other-worldly but a this-worldly religion is commonly acknowledged. Although Sufism and other allied factors in medieval centuries had altered this perspective, the positivistic shift in the later reform movements is, in itself, a phenomenon of remarkable significance. The Muslim's view became focused again on moral issues, and social ailments and their remedies are considered in the light of their conformity to God's law.

Nevertheless, the term "Islamic positivism," as we have applied it to these reform phenomena, is merely intended to signify the reformers' preoccupation with the situation of Islamic societies *in this world* and their proposed remedy in terms of "obedience to God's law." It has little to do with the modern Western concept of positivism which denies transcendence and seeks to base moral values on an empirical foundation. The positivism of these Islamic reform movements, on the other hand, was thoroughly transcendentalist; here they differ not only from Western positivism but from Ibn Khaldun as well. Western positivism became so empirical that it began to shy away from any talk of morality, and the very term "moral law" or "principle" seemed to it to be hopelessly "metaphysical." But the positivism of these Islamic movements came to be so transcendentally anchored that its idea of "obedience to God's law" was absolutely literalist. This concept threatened to reduce Islam to the barest bones; in the eyes of these reformers, empirical data would contaminate God's law, and therefore must have no relevance to it.

All the movements led by these reformers—whether the Arabian, the Indian, the Libyan, the Nigerian or the Sudanese—sought the reassertion of original, unadulterated Islam. In their view, Islam had become contaminated by historical accretions and foreign influences, and their attention therefore was fixed on the Koran and the sunnah (example) of the Prophet. These are the only definitive sources in Islam since all the other theological, doctrinal, or legal views represented in medieval schools lacked basic authority. What these two sources contain is a pure and absolute monotheism that had been dangerously compromised by the acceptance of sufi doctrines and practices that inculcated veneration of God's creatures and promoted such things as pilgrimages to the tombs of saints and cults and rituals woven around real or imagined holy men.

IJTIHAD—INTELLECTUAL INTERPRETATION

But if the sources of true Islam were the Koran and the sunnah alone, how could Muslims recover the original message? On this point, all of these reformist movements emphasized the concept of *ijtihad*, a term taken from the classical legal thought of Islam which means to exert one's intellectual powers to find answers to problems. Since the "problem" before Muslims was how to shed the burden of *shirk* (the association of partners with God which the Koran denounces as the most heinous sin), they had to think for themselves to rediscover the monotheistic message of the Koran that sufism had overlaid with degrading beliefs and practices. Muslims, the reformers urged, must not hearken to any voice other than the original sources of Islam.

Ijtihad was meant to do more than solve new problems by using historical Islamic roots and reason together: it was to reenact Islam at its historical roots. In India, for example, the collapse of Muslim political power created a new situation which the Indian movement attempted to solve, but this demanded *jihad* (holy war) rather than *ijtihad* and the *jihad* failed; this was also the case with the Mahdi in the Sudan. In the Arabian Peninsula, although *ijtihad* was doctrinally emphasized, *jihad* was used to purify Islam of all vestiges of *shirk*.

There is no doubt that this insistence on the responsibility of Muslims to think for themselves and not to accept uncritically any post-Prophetic authority was a great liberating force in a community that had become encumbered by so much dead weight in law and by the deadening drug of the popular religion. What these movements bequeathed to Islam was vibrant reawakening of will and purpose, an impatience with its *status quo* of slothful superstition, and, gradually, a sense of a meaningful unity as a global community. But at the same time, they left on Islam the mark of their limited objectives and vision. Since the leaders of these movements were interested in negating some of the influence of the medieval schools of Islamic thought and law, they inevitably took a negative attitude toward the intellectual and spiritual developments that had taken place in the intervening centuries. While it is true that the traditional system of *madrasah* education had become stagnant and had produced little original thought in the later medieval centuries, it is equally true that before stagnation set in, it had gained a high level of sophistication and a richness of content that was superior to that of its Western contemporaries. These reform movements, in their revivalist zeal, over-simplified the educational curriculum to such an extent that they starved themselves intellectually. It is this intellectual poverty which stifled the very spirit of *ijtihad*.

THE MODERNISTS

But if these early revivalists were unwilling or unable to do much by way of *ijtihad*, the more forward lands of the Muslim world—Turkey, Egypt, and the Indian subcontinent—gave birth (about the middle of the nineteenth century) to the phenomenon of Islamic modernism whose representatives wrote a brilliant new chapter in the history of Islamic thought. The essence of this new thought was the creation of positive links between the thought of the Koran and modern thought at certain key points, resulting in the integration of modern institutions with the moral-social orientation of the Koran. This intellectual effort, undertaken by several outstanding thinkers, is based on the legacy of the eighteenth and nineteenth century revivalist movements, i.e., on the twin principles that the Koran and the Prophet's example are the sole determinants of Islam and that Muslims are duty-bound to find solutions to new problems through *ijtihad* on the basis of those principles.

The great difference between the situation of the premodernist revivalists (or fundamentalists) and that of the modernists is that whereas the revivalists either did not find much that needed to be resolved by *ijtihad*, or were unwilling to exercise it, the modernists confronted entirely new situations which they were bold enough to attempt to resolve. Intellectually, the modernists experienced the ferment that resulted from the impact of certain important modern Western ideas on the Islamic tradition. This new intellectual agitation concerned issues ranging from the relationship of faith to reason, through political and social questions, and eventually to economic problems.

Since Muslim modernists essentially were representatives of Islamic liberalism, their activity involved individual thought; unlike fundamentalism, it did not take the form of a popular movement. But from this fact one must not jump to the conclusion, as many contemporary Western writers have done with respect to the current resurgence of neo-fundamentalism, that modernism was inherently weak. Indeed, several Western writers have thought that Islamic modernism was an external phenomenon generated by the impact of Western thought on Islam, and that it is dead now. That this view is superficial and shortsighted should become clear from the following account of what Islamic modernism stands for, what the contemporary rise of fundamentalism means, and how the two are mutually related.

THE MODERNISTS: METHODOLOGY

It is essential to grasp the methodology of classical modernism to discover its inherent strength and to be able to appreciate where it needs improvement. First of all, as we have indicated, it worked within the broad framework advocated by the premodernist revivalist movements, i.e., to accept only the Koran and the Sunnah as definitive and to withhold such acceptance from the later medieval developments in Islam. True, many modernists drew upon certain phenomena in medieval Islam as sources of inspiration and of support for their own positions, for example, the flowering of Islamic science and philosophy from the tenth to the thirteenth century. But this was because they saw the frequent Koranic injunctions to man to think, to reflect, to use his reason, and to exploit nature for beneficial human ends as embodied in that part of their history. They assailed Western critics of Islam's backwardness, pointing out that this backwardness was due to the fact that Muslims had deviated from Islam and neglected its invitation to think, whereas the West had made scientific and other progress only when it had rebelled against the tyranny of the medieval church over the human mind.

It was here that the modernist parted company with the early fundamentalist who, although he had undoubtedly emphasized the use of reason, had done so only for limited objectives. The fundamentalist did not think of science at all; he thought of philosophy, but took such fright at certain doctrines of the Muslim medieval philosophers, particularly those of al-Farabi (870–950) and Ibn Sina (980–1037) that to teach and study philosophy seemed to him to be counted among the most heinous of sins and the greatest perversion of human thought. It was mainly this perception that prompted the revivalist to simplify his educational curriculum and starve Muslims intellectually. But the modernist reopened the question of the relationship of faith and reason, and asked whether reason had limits or whether it could sit in judgment on faith.

This departure from the literalism of the earlier revivalists was facilitated by the modernists' use of an important intellectual approach: the effort to discover the spirit or the objectives of the Koranic teaching rather than holding mechanically to its literal meaning. The intellectual activity of the modernist was primarily in the field of social problems, i.e., in the areas of political thought, education, rights of women, and later, in economics. In all these areas, the modernist gave Islam a liberal interpretation and advocated changes in medieval Islamic institutions, doctrines, and practices.

Thus, in the political field, the modernist based himself on the Koranic statement that enjoins Muslims to govern their affairs by "mutual consultation" (*shura*). On this ground, he repudiated the legitimacy in Islam of kings, sultans, and all forms of autocratic or quasi-autocratic rule. He demanded the setting up of constitutional forms of governement with democratic institutions manned by the elected representatives of the people, and contended that this was the most effective way of implementing the Koranic principle of *shura*. The modernist's contention played a key role in the Muslim world, The issue is still far from resolved, however; indeed, democracy lately has faced fresh obstacles, in addition to those from Islamic conservatives and fundamentalists and from those who feel that democracy hinders the rapid economic development the Third World countries desperately need.

THE MODERNISTS: EDUCATION

In the field of educational reform, the modernist insisted that the exclusion of the rational and empirical sciences from the curriculum of the traditional educational system and the emphasis on what were called the "Shariah sciences" or the "religious disciplines" was unwarranted and harmful, and that educational policies excluding these sciences were responsible for Muslim backwardness in the scientific field. The modernists were able to set up seats of modern learning, despite opposition from the conservatives in the initial stages, and today these new institutions are flourishing all over the Muslim world. Generally speaking, the main problem in this today is not a lack of modern educational apparatus, but rather a lack of creative synthesis and of an organic relationship between the traditional-religious and the modern-secular. The institutions of traditional and modern learning are for the most part brutally juxtaposed, and produce two types of people who can hardly communicate with each other. We shall see presently how this educational dichotomy has produced the neo-fundamentalism currently in ascendance in the Muslim world.

THE MODERNISTS: WOMEN'S RIGHTS

On the question of the rights of women, the modernist contended that the Koran had not only improved their status but had granted them virtually equal rights with men. Some even claimed that the Koran made women the equal of men in all essential respects, that certain inequalities that had existed in Islam were largely due to social custom—much of which was anti-Islamic—and that some of these inequalities were due to misperceptions of the purposes of the Koran by medieval Muslim lawyers. Modernists thus distinguished between the principles, values, or objectives of the Koran, on the one hand, and some of its legal solutions, on the other.

THE MODERNISTS: ECONOMICS

On the economic side, the modernists advocated the acceptance of modern banking practices on grounds that the institution of *riba* (interest), banned by the Koran, was a grossly oppressive and exploitative usurious system that could not be identified with today's bank interest. However, on the question of economic justice, the record of Islamic modernism is generally rather poor.

Muslim modernists have seldom seen economic justice as a serious problem, and this question has burst into the forefront since the 1950s and 1960s. There is no doubt that both monotheism and economic justice were pivotal to the Koran, but it is one of the mysteries of subsequent developments that, while monotheism was well-remembered, economic justice largely fell into oblivion. It is only recently that some Muslim leaders—for example, Qadhafi and Khomeini—have restored it to the center of Islamic ideology.

WEAKNESSES IN THE MODERNIST POSITION

On the whole, the position of the modernists on the several issues briefly outlined here is respectable, and their theses command an inherent plausibility as testimony to intellectual innovation. The modernist was sincere, but his work suffered from two drawbacks. First, his approach to an interpretation of the Koran was selective. He did not make an effort explicitly to formulate a methodology for a systematic and comprehensive interpretation of the Koran and the sunnah in order to guide the moral and legal teaching of Islam and to correct some of the shortcomings and excesses of the classical systems of Islam. He treated only those questions that impinged on this consciousness as demanding solutions. Second, some modernists showed an alarming tendency toward apologetics on crucial matters, particularly when interpreting Islamic history. For example, in view of Western criticisms of Islam on the issue of *jihad* and the slogan that "Islam was spread by the sword," many tried to show that all the Prophet's wars and the wars of the early Muslims were purely defensive.

These two weaknesses—coupled with the fact that many modernists advocated the adoption not only of modern democracy, science, and education, but also of Western social mores—resulted in a rejection of modernism by the new forces that began to take shape during the early years of this century. The modernist aroused suspicion even about his loyalty to Islam, and he was accused of being a pale reflection of the West and of sacrificing Islam at its altar. His critics asked whether the exploitation by Western colonialism was better than the Islamic *jihad*, which at least taught egalitarianism to mankind, and whether Western methods for acquiring economic markets and profits were superior to early Islamic ways, which at least had the moral objective of establishing an ethical social order. These critics of the West and of Islamic modernism pointed their fingers at the breakdown of Western social mores, particularly at the danger to which the institution of the family was exposed. If these were the consequences of the freedom of women, Muslims had better think twice before imitating it.

By the mid-1930s, there had appeared a new generation of young men and women keen to settle scores with the West. The communist world did not invade their consciousness. Russia might be the greatest imperialist power, but its brute force was beyond anything the Muslims could match, and they could only hope that the communist system's grave violation of human nature would lead to its self-destruction. The West, however, claimed to stand for human values, though it consistently flouted them, so that Muslims could encounter the West on the same wave length.

CONTRAST BETWEEN TRADITIONALISTS AND
NEO-FUNDAMENTALISTS

In the ensuing analysis, we shall speak of four groups among Muslims—the secularist, the modernist, the traditionalist, and the neo-fundamentalist, this last term applying to the organized groups emerging in the 1930s. Since the secularist stand—seeking to separate religion from state and effected in Turkey since the 1920s—has been generally discredited by Muslims at the theoretical level, we will omit it from the present treatment. The lines between some modernists and secularists may be rather vague, however, since there are modernists who espouse Western norms. But a distinction between the early fundamentalist-traditionalist-conservative, and what we have called the neo-fundamentalist is important to make, even though there has been interaction between the two.

The first contrast between the traditionalist-conservative *alim* (a man learned in the law and Islamic studies) and the neo-fundamentalist is that the former is rooted in a tradition; he bears the burden of it; he defends it and is a spokesman for it. This tradition certainly goes back to the Koran and the Prophet, but there is no tradition which represents its cited original source uniquely, exhaustively, or faithfully. The Koran itself challenged the faithfulness of Jewish and Christian traditions to the sources which they claimed. For the traditionalist there is no new age in the real sense of the word. For him, the Koran has no other meaning than what his tradition has determined. His tradition, in fact, is the only mirror through which he can see the message of the Koran. It is against this that the early, premodernist fundamentalist had risen in revolt, and against this that the contemporary neo-fundamentalist has arisen in challenge.

One important difference between the two outlooks, despite their commonality of purpose, is that traditional conservatism had a much narrower base, while neo-fundamentalism, since it is postmodernist and has been influenced by modernism, is a modern, richer version of fundamentalism.

This is why we have called it neo-fundamentalism. While traditional conservatism arose from within the Islamic tradition, neo-fundamentalism is very much a response to foreign influences and pressures. Neo-fundamentalism, then, may be defined as *an Islamic bid to rediscover the original meaning of the Islamic message without historic deviations and distortions and without being encumbered by the intervening tradition, this bid being meant not only for the benefit of the Islamic community but as a challenge to the world and to the West in particular.*

From this perspective, then, as we remarked about earlier fundamentalist movements, neo-fundamentalism is a liberating force, freeing the mind both from centuries of tradition and from the intellectual and spiritual domination of the West. Neo-fundamentalism also talks loudly and incessantly about *ijtihad.* Unfortunately, however, as we have watched its career during the past half century, *ijtihad* had been marking time; in this respect, the actual performance of neo-fundamentalism has been considerably poorer than that of the earlier fundamentalism. For earlier fundamentalist movements had at least produced something new in the stale atmosphere of traditionalism by focusing attention on the authority of the Koran and the Prophet, procedurally, and on the monotheism of the Koran, substantively. But as successor to the *ijtihad* of modernism, the performance of neo-fundamentalism is generally negative. The basic reason for this intellectual poverty is that neo-fundamentalism came as a reaction to modernism and to what was perceived as the excessively pro-Western orientation of most modernists. So long as the central feature of the character of neo-fundamentalism remains reactionary, it will not generate positive intellectual results, no matter how much it may talk of *ijtihad.* A closer analysis reveals that two factors are responsible for this situation.

SHORTCOMINGS OF NEO-FUNDAMENTALISM

We have noted that the qualitative performance of neo-fundamentalism is much poorer than that of many earlier fundamentalists and modernists. This is not fortuitous. For the founders of earlier movements were themselves products of the traditional education system. They were thoroughly trained *ulema* who had become dissatisfied with the status quo and who worked for a change. They were rooted in a tradition which, however stagnant it had become, was still rich and intellectually capable of cultivating a depth and dignity of personality. Once they revolted against tradition, therefore, they knew what they wanted to achieve, and what the stakes were. The neo-fundamentalist, on the contrary, is generally *not* rooted in the tradition. He has had little traditional education and, in fact, does not know what the tradition is. Although Islam has no priesthood, it has persons who have specialized in Islamic jurisprudence and theology. The neo-fundamentalist, once he decided to get rid of traditional encumbrances, succeeded in getting rid of *all* tradition. There is no one among the fundamentalists that I know of—with the exception of Ayatollah Khomeini—who is a well-trained *alim* in the traditional sense. So far as Islamic learning is concerned, they are dilettantes: indeed, neo-fundamentalism is basically a function of laymen, many of whom are professionals—lawyers, doctors, engineers.

Many of the modernists were also laymen, but many of the most influential modernists were religiously trained scholars. These were men who went through powerful intellectual agitation with the firm conviction that, with honest intellectual effort, problems facing Muslims could be solved on the basis of understanding and interpreting the principles of Islam. Neo-fundamentalism, on the other hand, seems to think it has a divine mission to shut down Islamic intellectual life. Its insistence on Islam as a practical undertaking in which intellectualism without a link to the world of the practical is only a form of intellectual alcoholism is correct. But its assumption that Muslims can straighten out the practical world without serious intellectual effort, with the aid only of catchy slogans, is a dangerous mistake. Not only have neo-fundamentalists failed to seek new insights into Islam through broadening their intellectual horizons, they have even let go the richness of traditional learning.

ISLAM AND COLONIALISM

A basic factor in this situation is undoubtedly the colonial experience of Muslim societies which appears to have created a psychological hiatus in the Muslim mind. The Muslim mind seems to be appalled at suggestions that there may be a better way of understanding a certain issue than our forefathers might have thought of. The shaken self-confidence balks at a mildly innovative idea, yet in the precolonial age Muslims have sometimes expressed ideas far more radical than those over which a storm would arise today.

The colonial phenomenon is not something only of the past; it appears to be continuing indefinitely. Political and military imperialism was bad enough, but more heinous is the ethical, cultural, and intellectual arrogance of the West. In the past, all ascendant civilizations have had their moments of self-righteousness, but probably no civilization before that of the modern West has felt itself to be so universally and comprehensively valid that the mere questioning of some of its values can be tantamount to barbaric backwardness. It may make economic animals of its own members in the name of civilized values; it may talk of equality and freedom at home, but perpetrate gross economic exploitation abroad. Its conscience, hypersensitive to infringements of human rights, not only suffered little disturbance over, but sponsored, the expulsion of the Palestinian Arabs from their homes and their land to make room for a new phenomenon, the authentic child of this very conscience. Nor are the valiant Afghan freedom fighters, engaged in a life and death struggle against the brutal Russian invasion of their homeland, beneficiaries as yet of defensive weapons from the Western powers.

THE ISLAMIC FUTURE

The question, however, is: Do Muslims become more effective or constructive by becoming psychologically so entangled with the West that they seem to be paralyzed when it comes to reconstructing their own societies on Islamic lines? It is the zeal to demonstrate Islam's distinctiveness from the West that is responsible for the futile search for a system of interest-free banking. Hardly any notice is taken of the terrible forms of economic exploitation and fraudulent trade practices like gross profiteering, hoarding, adulteration of food, as though the Koran and the sunnah are silent on these points. What kind of man does the Koran aim at producing? If this question can be successfully answered by Muslims, all questions can be answered.

If this question cannot be answered, the Muslim must occupy himself with certain selected aspects of conventional belief and practice and a pathological preoccupation with exhibiting the great masterpiece that Islam once was—in the fields of science, philosophy, literature, and art. Certainly, the Muslim's concern over the influence of the decaying Western sense of values on Muslim society is genuine. But here again, the solution lies in finding out what kind of human personality the Koran wants to mold, primarily in the home and in the school, and not simply in putting veils on women.

But whatever we have said about the negative aspects of neo-fundamentalism—its lack of a viable methodology, or indeed, of any methodology at all for the interpretation of Islam, the absence of an integral vision of Islam, and the general poverty of its intellectual content—must not make us oblivious to its intensity. It is vibrant, it pulsates with anger and enthusiasm, and it is exuberant and full of righteous hatred. Its ethical dynamism is genuine, its integrity remarkable. Some of its expressions may be disconcerting or even grotesque, but should it find enough content, it could prove to be a great, even decisive, force in a world torn by individual, national, racist, and communal selfishness and narrowmindedness, and for a humanity wounded by mutual exploitation, inhuman aggression, and chronic mistrust. This must, at any rate, remain the hope.

Part 1

Modernization and Tradition

*C*HE DEEPEST, MOST PERSISTENT PROBLEMS FACING MUSLIM STATES TODAY are those related to the modernizing or simply the adapting of societies to the increasingly pressing requirements of a changing world. The seven essays which comprise this section discuss the ways in which several diverse nations, stretching half way around the globe, are dealing with these problems. The authors who write about Iran, Pakistan, the Sudan, and Malaysia are citizens of those countries, while the other essays are written by knowledgeable foreigners. The countries they write about, taken collectively, present examples of the range of problems, strengths and weaknesses that are typical of many Muslim nations today, as well as the ways in which each nation is influenced by its Islamic heritage. The nations discussed in this section are all Muslim, but their experiences and their approaches to their problems do not and cannot constitute a compendium of Islamic reaction to the modern world. Every Muslim country has its own character, derived in part from its pre-Islamic and colonial history, and these histories are as distinct as those of non-Muslim countries.

All but two of the nations discussed in this section (Egypt and Iran), like the majority of Muslim states, became independent only after the end of World War II, following a century or more of experience as colonies or clients of a West European state. A majority were led to independence, usually after some degree of violence, by men who were in large part Western educated and who had incorporated into their own thinking such Western concepts as nationalism and material progress. In the early years of independence, these ideas in their more heady forms tended to be used and expounded by most national leaders as basic to the process which became known as "nation-building."

One of the main objectives of the nationalistic/materialistic approach is to give to the citizen of the new nation a feeling of dignity and importance resulting from that citizenship and from his ethnic origin, and to make him feel different from and superior to a citizen of another nation, even if both are Muslims. Islam, which is based on the equality of the faithful in the sight of God and on social doctrines which are both antiracist and antimaterialist, tends to lead in very different directions. Religious leaders, therefore, were generally not influential in the organization of independence in most of the new Muslim states. In fact, the leadership in most countries emphasized religion as a rallying point only where people of a different religion were perceived as a threat to the new state, as in Pakistan and Malaysia.

This pattern of secular thinking, nationalism, and emphasis on material progress has continued to dominate the plans and actions of most governments in the Muslim world. In the past few years, however, the initial euphoria of independence has worn off. Material progress has lagged or has not brought the new era of happiness expected of it. Above all, new generations of educated or partly educated young people who have no personal recollecton of colonialism have found that the world seems to have no place for them.

It is understandable that large numbers of these young people, mostly urban, and the poorer classes, rural and urban, whose lives have not witnessed great improvement over the past years, should begin to conclude that there must be a better way and that it must be sought through a return to the teachings of Islam—a return to the basic values from which the fact of political independence had deflected their attention. This feeling in many countries is challenging the newer, but essentially imported, ideas about what is most important that have been put forward by the still dominant secular modernists.

This challenge runs through the Muslim world as a common theme with wide national variations. In the present period it is a major source of concern for the leaders of Muslim states. It also has consequences for the West, for challenge to or rejection of Western concepts inevitably leads to doubts about and suspicion of relationships with the West, particularly with the United States.

It is worth noting that there is no indication in the following essays that there yet exists anything resembling a serious or coordinated attempt by anyone but the Ayatollah Khomeini to orchestrate or internationalize these national movements for a return to religion. It seems, rather, at least to date, that the primary motivation has been dissatisfaction with life as it has developed after three decades or more of basically secular independence.

3

ᴐ̃ran

THE "ISLAMIC CULTURAL REVOLUTION"

Rouhollah K. Ramazani

Ｄｕｒｉｎｇ the week of the ill-fated Ａｍｅｒｉｃａｎ rescue mission of April 24, 1980, Iran launched its "cultural revolution." This event occurred during the bloody riots at the universities in Tehran, Meshed, Shiraz, and Isfahan, which resulted in the deaths of some 26 Iranians and injuries to many more. Reports in the American press implied that the Revolutionary Council's decree of April 18, 1980, had sparked the riots. The decree ordered the leftist student groups to close their campus offices and the universities to shut down earlier than scheduled in order to carry out a program of "Islamization." As a matter of fact, however, the Council's decree was issued after the students had already begun to take over universities and other institutions of higher learning.

The decree made no mention of a "cultural revolution" (*engelab-e farhangi*). Rather, it said that the Council's purpose was to make "basic transformations in the higher educational order" as soon as possible. On April 19, a day after the Council's decree, President Bani-Sadr used the phrase "cultural revolution," perhaps for the first time. In early May, a group of university, political, and other figures, including Masud Rajavi, leader of the *Mujahidin-e Khalq* ("People's Fighters"), met with Bani-Sadr for three days to discuss the "Islamic cultural revolution."

What is the meaning of this "cultural revolution?" Who launched it? Was it merely a device to use Islam for political ends, or was it a new, genuine attempt to relate the Islamic ideology of the revolutionary regime to the totality of Iranian culture? The revolution is still unfolding, and such subsequent developments as the election of the Parliament (*Majlis*), the formation of the first permanent government, and the release of the American hostages have done little to stabilize the new regime. On the contrary, the Iraqi attack on Iran (September 22, 1980) and its aftermath for the moment have overshadowed most other revolutionary activities, including the attempts at a cultural revolution. Yet the fact that such a revolution was proclaimed requires a brief discussion from the perspectives of ideology, politics, and culture.

Three components of the new Islamic ideology are most relevant. The first is the concept of a "unitized community." Neither the term "unified" nor "unitary" community can convey the meaning of the term as it is used in Iran's new constitution. The concept involves not only achieving the goal of a unified or unitary community but also the shaping of the community through ideological indoctrination. In the ambiguous language of the constitution: "From the viewpoint of Islam, the government does not arise from the notion of classes and mediation among persons or groups but is a crystallization of political idealism based on religious community and concord which provide its organization—which through the process of ideological transformation turns its path toward the final goal [movement toward God]." Such a "Government of God," to borrow the words of the Ayatollah Khomeini, perforce is entrusted with the task of shaping all aspects of Iranian life, including the cultural, according to the tenets of Islam as interpreted by the Ayatollah and his supporters and embodied in the new constitution.

A second component of the new Islamic ideology is the idea of the responsibility of "pious men" to rule and administer the nation on the basis of their interpretation of the Koran. These men create the political "positions and foundations" for shaping the society. But the "vanguard" of the Iranian revolution, according to the constitution, is the Ayatollah Khomeini, whose "centrality" as "the Islamic leader" was established and confirmed by the uprising of June 1963—"the starting point" of the current revolution. Underlying this leadership is the Twelver shii notion of the "deputyship of *al-Mahdi*" or the Twelfth Imam. This concept is not mentioned in the constitution, but it is embodied in its principles 5 and 110 which enumerate the leader's vast powers.

The third component is the abolition of the "idolatrous order." This notion referred initially to the rule and policies of the Pahlavi dynasty. Modernization, secularization, and the domestic and foreign policies of the late Shah and his father, as well as the role of those foreign powers that supported them, are considered to have been contrary to Khomeini's vision of Islam. The same view is now applied to any secular or religious individuals or groups that seem to deviate from the "Khomeini line."

The ideological rationale of this combative stance presumably is based on the Koranic injunction relating to the victory of the "oppressed" against the "oppressors." The Ayatollah Khomeini expressed the idea in his well-known declaration: "The oppressed people must triumph over the oppressors." The concepts of the "oppressed" and the "oppressors" both have been extended to individuals and collectivities of all types. For example, the late Shah and his close associates are "oppressors," while the masses are the "oppressed." At the international level, the superpowers, cartels, multinational corporations—in short, "capitalist imperialism and socialist imperialism" and their alleged "Zionist, Phalangist and Fascist" instruments—are examples of "oppressors." National liberation movements and many Third World countries fall into the category of the "oppressed."

Although the Khomeini ideology denounces both West and East as dominant blocs, the United States, in particular, is viewed as the "Great Satan," or the "principal enemy," for its past association with the "idolatrous" Shah and his "oppressive" policies. America is the only foreign country that is specifically denounced in the constitution. The alienation from the United States that now finds expression in ideology and practical policy is an integral part of a deeper and wider rejection of such perceived Western values as the primacy of individualism, as contrasted with Islamic communalism, and capitalism and materialism, as contrasted with Islamic welfarism and spiritualism. The presumed Pahlavi ideology of the late Shah and his father allegedly had led to the blind imitation of the West, or "Westomania" (*gharbzadegi*), a term more accurately translated as "hesperomania."

The first component discussed above—the "unitized community" that moves toward God—is the most fundamental aspect of Khomeini's Islamic ideology. Without it the other two, or any other aspect of the Khomeini ideology, cannot be properly understood. Once the divinely based unitized community is realized, all social, economic, political, and cultural inequalities and injustices at the individual, national, and international levels will disappear. This is what Khomeini calls "Islamic democracy," which, he believes, is superior to all other democracies. Only a divinely based unitized community can be truly democratic. Elimination of all foreign influences from every aspect of life, therefore, is regarded as essential to the development of an independent Islamic Iranian community.

President Bani-Sadr attempted to link the student riots and clashes between the government forces and the rebellious Kurds to the American rescue mission. He alleged that both were instigated by the United States to divert Iranian attention from the American military incursion. But in a more candid moment, before the rescue mission, he spoke against centers of power that rivaled the government, telling the students that the "first principle of this revolution is that the government elected by you must be the executive force of the people and no other executive force outside the government is justified in making the people's decisions."

Bani-Sadr probably moved quickly to obtain the support of the Ayatollah Khomeini and the Revolutionary Council for the idea of the "cultural revolution," which was endorsed by his rival, the Ayatollah Beheshti, in order to outflank the Muslim fundamentalist students who were allied with the captors of the American Embassy. Nevertheless, the leftist students, who were then dominant on most university campuses, viewed his move as an alignment with the right-wing Muslim students against them. It is likely that the right-wing Muslim students, allied with those who called themselves the followers of the "Khomeini line," started something like the idea of the "cultural revolution" and President Bani-Sadr chimed in.

The notion of the "cultural revolution" also had a wider political meaning. It represented yet another bid for power by the clerics as part of their effort to "clericalize" the revolutionary political process. In this sense, it may not have been what President Bani-Sadr really wanted, but the fundamentalist Muslim students took the initiative, not Bani-Sadr. They were going after the leftist groups in the universities, the *Fedayeen-e Khalq* (People's Sacrificers) and the *Mujahidin-e Khalq* (People's Fighters). Bani-Sadr tried to make the best of the situation by using the opportunity to reassert the limited and uncertain authority of the Presidency vis-a-vis the Ayatollah Beheshti and his supporters. From the perspective of the clerics, however, the dislodging of the leftist students from the campuses was a major triumph, for their student supporters had occupied fewer political headquarters in universities. The leftist students, after bloody resistance, were then forced to close their offices, and the Ayatollah Khomeini threatened to have the "masses" take over if the students failed to leave university premises.

The fundamentalist attack on the extremist left had seldom spared the moderate liberal elements. Leftists and liberals were both regarded as potential challengers to the clerics' effort to monopolize power, but the liberals less so. The leftists' sanctuaries in the universities had been largely established after they had been attacked by Muslim zealots in the summer of 1979. As a matter of fact, the struggle between the rightist students, on one hand, and liberal and leftist students, on the other, was part of a more basic cleavage between segments of the clerical and secular forces that had been allied in opposition to the late Shah before the seizure of power (February 10, 1979). The historic division between the two elements surfaced, as it had in the Constitutional Revolution (1905–11) and in the oil nationalization crisis (1951–53), only when the common enemy appeared defeated. Contrasted with these historical antecedents, however, the clerical leadership and its followers in this revolution had enjoyed unprecedented power from the beginning. Nevertheless, the Khomeini-Sanjabi understanding in France (November 1979) had acknowledged that the revolution was an embodiment of both the "national and Islamic movements."

Against this backdrop, the process of clericalization has been particularly painful for the secular elements because it has gone through four different stages since the revolutionary forces seized power.

First, although a referendum was held on the establishment of an Islamic Republic, critics opposed the lack of any choice besides the "Islamic Republic." Khomeini considered the referendum of secondary importance, believing that the revolution's success was an indication of the choice of the people. The opposition included some influential clergymen as well as secular elements. The Ayatollah Shariatmadari, as well as the National Front and other secular groups, criticized the lack of choice. The Frontists wished to include in the designation of the Republic the word "Democratic" but were unsuccessful: Khomeini and his supporters believed that Islam includes a democracy that is superior to those of both the Marxist-Leninist and the liberal-democratic varieties.

Second, the process of clericalization made a further gain with the adoption of the new constitution. A "Constituent Assembly" had been promised, but an "Assembly of Experts" was elected. The critics objected to this method for it substituted some 75 representatives for the 300 who would have been otherwise elected. The small number of representatives and other devices insured the dominance of the fundamentalist clergy in the Assembly. More important, the critics objected to the extensive powers of the *faqih* (the Twelfth Imam's deputy) under the constitution, arguing that the will of the people as a God-given right should not be frustrated.

Third, the Ayatollah Khomeini's exclusion of the clerics from the presidential candidacy was not a significant gain for the other forces. In the first place, the President enjoyed quite limited powers under the constitution; second, even the landslide victory of President Bani-Sadr could not make much difference in the wielding of real power. The clergy-dominated Islamic Revolutionary Council and the Muslim fundamentalist captors of the American Embassy, in addition to the Ayatollah Khomeini, were already on the scene as formidable power centers when the new Parliament was elected. Bani-Sadr enjoyed the confidence of the Imam, but this was not enough to counterbalance the other contending forces, as evidenced by his repeated failure to have the Ayatollah on his side when the chips were down. Within the Revolutionary Council, which Bani-Sadr chaired, he faced formidable rivals, especially Beheshti; outside the Council he was rebuffed by the students in the American Embassy. They embarrassed Bani-Sadr politically, for example, by blocking the visit of the United Nations mission to the American Embassy in Tehran which he had arranged and by foiling his efforts to arrange for the transfer of the custody of the hostages to Iranian authorities. Khomeini, in the end, supported the students in both cases.

Finally, the process of clericalization was dramatically capped by the election of the large number of clerical deputies to the Majlis and the appointment of Rajai, a fundamentalist layman, as Prime Minister. The Beheshti-Bani-Sadr power struggle was now overshadowed by bitter differences between Rajai and Bani-Sadr over policy, personnel, and ideology. They could not, for example, agree on the selection of several key cabinet ministers.

Bani-Sadr tried to use his temporary position as Commander-in-Chief, especially after the outbreak of the Iraq-Iran war, as a means of resisting the attacks of his opponents and of building a new base of power. His opponents, however, blamed him for the military's lack of success in defending Iran against Iraq. In retaliation, Bani-Sadr, who had been an early supporter of a quick settlement of the hostage dispute, blamed the Rajai government for having made an unfavorable agreement with the United States. Just as the taking of American hostages had been mainly a political move, their release was also linked to the struggle for power among the revolutionary politicians.

Thus, from a political perspective, the launching of the cultural revolution represented a major political move by the fundamentalist Muslim clerics and their lay supporters to insure their preeminence in the emerging political order. From an ideological standpoint, the cultural revolution reflected their desire to insure the purity of the new order's ideological foundation in terms of the tenets of Islamic fundamentalism as interpreted primarily by the Ayatollah Khomeini and his close associates. The ideological and political success of the clergy in creating the new order would guarantee, it was believed, the defeat of the "counterrevolutionaries." This term meant any individual, group, or state perceived as opposing the prescriptions of the revolutionary purists, or as being too critical even if not in opposition to the regime. The proposed new shii ideology that was first used to delegitimize the Pahlavi dynasty and its ideology was now formally adopted in the new constitution, and the clerical "vanguards" of the ideology now controlled the new political and legal institutions. But the challenge of competing ideologies and political forces to the emerging new order continued unabated.

In June 1981, the basic power struggle underpinning the Islamic "cultural revolution" in Iran resulted in the dismissal of Bani-Sadr by the Ayatollah Khomeini. The ideological and cultural as well as political components of this struggle, as this goes to press (July 1981), are being played out even more violently than the Revolution's earlier phase. The final outcome is still in doubt.

The attempt at an Islamic "cultural revolution" should be viewed also from a cultural perspective for the important reason that the Ayatollah Khomeini himself did so. In a major speech on April 21, 1980, he denied that the notion of a "cultural revolution" simply meant the future establishment of educational programs at Iranian universities based on the study of classical Islamic subjects or the discontinuation of teaching of "modern science." He declared that "the meaning of Islamization of universities is that they will be emancipated from the West and the East so that we can have an independent nation, an independent university and an independent culture." With an eye to the hostage crisis and the United States at the same time, he added: "We are not afraid of economic sanctions and military intervention. What frightens us is cultural dependency. We are afraid of universities that train our youth to serve the West or Communism."

In other words, culturally, ideologically, and politically, alien values must be rejected in favor of Islamic values; that is the basic requirement of an "independent culture." But the underlying question is how the new Islamic cultural values are to be related to the totality of Iranian culture. To put it differently, will Islam be interpreted broadly or narrowly? As noted above, the fundamentalist interpretation of Islam has been formally embodied in the new constitution. And the fundamentalist forces have managed to dominate the newly emergent political and legislative processes. But there is no comparable revolutionary experience in the cultural field. Hence, it is difficult to predict whether the fundamentalist interpretation will prevail in the cultural field as well.

Yet the Islamization of Iranian culture will present the most difficult challenge of all. The reason for this is that, in the ideological and political fields, the inherent contradictions in Iran's past experiments had been acknowledged widely; thus their rejection seemed easier. The constitutional formula of the early twentieth century embodied competing ideas of shiism, nationalism, monarchism, and democratic liberalism. The Pahlavi formula added the conflicting ideas of absolutist monarchism and socioeconomic welfarism (the "White Revolution") without any genuine attempt at democratic liberalization of the polity. The late Shah's attempts, and those of his father, at economic, social, legal, and military modernization were, in the final analysis, the legitimizing instruments of their regimes. Once the socioeconomic crumbs distributed to the public no longer counterbalanced the long-standing political alienation, the legitimacy of the regime and its ideology were challenged by disparate revolutionary forces. Their conflicting ideologies ranged from fundamentalist shiism, to Islamic-socialism, Marxist-

Leninism, orthodox communism, and nationalist liberalism. But their common opposition to the late Shah's regime united them in their revolutionary struggle until its downfall. The present preeminence of fundamentalist shiism, both ideologically and politically, is now challenged by many of the same forces that had been previously the allies of the fundamentalist shii clerics.

A narrow interpretation of shii Islam—as applied to Iranian culture—would challenge both the cultural values underlying the ideologies of the disparate revolutionary forces and the Persian component of Iranian culture. The superficial Pahlavi synthesis of the pre-Islamic and Western cultural values should not overshadow the fundamental historical and cultural fact that cultural values in Iran contain both Persian and Islamic characteristics. The failure of the Pahlavi rulers to take serious note of the Islamic component of the culture partly explains the "resurgence of Islam" under deteriorating social, economic, and political conditions. Would not the application of a fundamentalist and narrow interpretation of Shii Islam, in effect, amount to a denial of the Persian component of Iranian culture?

This is not a hypothetical question because historically Iranian cultural and national identity was not totally replaced by Islam. In embracing Islam after the Arab conquest in the seventh century, Iranians rejected a narrow interpretation of Islam. They rejected the Umayyad Arabization of Islam and introduced, especially under Abbasid rule, Iranian values into every major aspect of the emerging Islamic civilization, so much so that outstanding scholars of Islamic and Iranian cultures have dubbed the development as the "Persian conquest of Islam." This is no exercise in hyperbole, as evidenced by the enduring Iranian influence in Islamic arts, literature, politics, philosophy, medicine, architecture, and other fields. Above all, this is attested by the rejection of Arabic and the revival of Persian as the symbol of Persian literary renaissance and Iranian national and cultural identity centuries before the rise of modern Iran at the turn of the sixteenth century. The adoption at that time of shiism as the state religion has never been widely considered as a denial of the Persian component of the Iranian culture.

Two traditional values of the Islamic-Iranian culture stand out as a result of this broad interpretation of Islam as it relates to the totality of the culture. One is cosmopolitanism. Such internationally renowned poets as Ferdowsi, Hafiz, Omar Khayyam and Saadi, and such architectural gems as the Masjid-e Shah (Mosque of the Shah) and the Masjid-e Shaikh Lutfullah in Isfahan belong to world civilization. Historically, Islamic universalism has its parallel in pre-Islamic Iranian cosmopolitanism as evidenced, for example, by the Persian absorption of Egyptian, Mesopotamian, Elamite, Greek, and other ancient influences in the magnificent architectural monuments at Persepolis, Parsargadae, and Susa.

The other traditional Islamic-Iranian cultural value that would be even more relevant in our increasingly interdependent world is humanitarianism, although it is in eclipse in Iran today. There are no lines that better capture the Islamic-Iranian concern with humanity than the admonition of the thirteenth century Iranian poet, Saadi:

> The sons of men are members in a body whole related,
> For of a single essence are they and all created. When
> Fortune persecutes with pain one member sorely, surely
> The other members of the body cannot stand securely. O
> You who from another's trouble turn aside your view, It
> Is not fitting they bestow the name of "Man" on you!

4

Egypt

ISLAM AND SOCIAL CHANGE

John Waterbury

*A*T THE START OF THE 1980s, as it has for the past millennium, Islam retains its central position in the social, cultural, political, and symbolic life of Egypt. Nevertheless, Islam has felt the pressure of drastic social and political change. Since the early nineteenth century, Islam, as doctrine and social institution, has been challenged by foreign political dominance, alien social customs, and Western learning. The new elite brought to power by the 1952 Revolution has attempted to put Islam, its institutions, and its hold over the emotions of the people to new uses in the process of nation building and political mobilization.

Because of its profound importance to Egyptians, Islam has been at once a cause of dissension and a source of unity. For the pious, it offers an answer to the complicated problems of a stalemated society. As always, its message is faith and integrity; its fiber, the failure of the dominant order on the battlefield and in solving economic and social problems. The same message can be adapted to new problems—peace, economic crises, the corruption of public officials.

The call of fundamentalist Muslims has resonance because it invites participation, an invitation that contrasts with the official political regimen which reduces citizens to spectators. At a time many Egyptians feel confused and find themselves facing an uncertain future, Islamic fundamentalism connects them to a tradition that reduced bewilderment. Islam taught men and women to struggle for worthwhile causes; it also taught that the faithful can rediscover the will to persevere and the capacity for patience. The importance and the power of Islamic fundamentalism lie in its ability to destabilize a regime and to help bring it down by denying it the religious mantle that remains an important source of political power.

The 1952 Revolution is instructive. The Moslem Brotherhood helped to topple the monarchy, but it soon became the victim of the new regime. Fundamentalism supplied the fervor, some of the committed manpower, and the willingness to take risks. But other actors more capable of making compromises inherited post-revolutionary Egypt. Despite their differences in approach, both Nasser and Sadat seem to have proceeded from an accurate reading of Islamic and Egyptian constraints and possibilities.

THE SOCIETY

Egypt is a very old and highly integrated society that has been portrayed as set in its ways. It is true that Egypt's long history of peasant-based agriculture, strong centralized government, and ethnic homogeneity have imbued it with a sense of collective identity and nationhood that is replicated nowhere else in the Middle East. It is likewise true that this sense of self makes Egypt resistant to rapid change and resilient in the face of it.

But rapid change there has been. While Egypt may weather its buffeting better than many of its neighbors, change has produced severe strains in the social fabric. In the space of seventy years, the population grew from 11.1 millions (1907) to 36.6 millions (1976 census). The per capita availability of land dropped from .5 acres to .15 acres. Dwindling land resources abetted a massive shift of population from the countryside to the cities; over the same seventy-year period the proportion of the total population living in urban areas rose from 19 percent to 44 percent. In 1976, over 16 million people were crowded into Egypt's cities, nearly half of them in Greater Cairo.

While impressive inroads were made into mass illiteracy in the twentieth century, 56 percent of all Egyptians over the age of ten were illiterate in 1976 (42 percent of all males and 71 percent of all females). More striking, the rapid rate of population growth meant that, while the proportion of illiterates declined, the absolute numbers of them increased to over 15 million in 1976. That figure is considerably larger that the total Egyptian population of 1907. This pool of uneducated, generally unskilled persons has placed a tremendous burden on the Egyptian economy as it tries to shift from an agricultural to an industrial base.

But even the educated and literate have proved a mixed blessing. Under the Nasser regime after 1952, the public educational system was expanded at all levels. There are now over six million Egyptians enrolled in primary and secondary schools, technical institutes, and universities. The latter two turn out over 100,000 graduates each year. For nearly two decades, the Egyptian state has acted as the employer of last resort for any university graduate or equivalent thereof. In 1970, it was estimated that 60 percent of all living university graduates were in public employ.

The results, while perhaps laudable from the viewpoint of social equity, have been close to disastrous in terms of administrative performance. The civil service has swollen to over two million, and public sector enterprises employ well over one million. If the armed forces, police and school teachers are included, nearly half of the active work force probably is on the public payroll, and most of the other half is engaged in agriculture. What is left is the private sector, non-agricultural work force, perhaps a million strong, scattered among tens of thousands of small-scale enterprises, and the petty tradesmen, street vendors, scavengers, muleteers and the like.

Thus the Egyptian state apparatus has become a monolith, laden with unneeded personnel (labor redundancy in the public sector is estimated at about 30 percent of the total workforce) and bogged down in paper and complicated routines. Salaries generally are so low that civil servants often moonlight to make ends meet.

Egypt's challenge in this century has been to provide, with limited land resources and raw materials, a decent standard of living for a burgeoning population. The dynasty that had ruled Egypt throughout the nineteenth century in the name of the Ottoman Sultan and then until 1952 under the direct or indirect aegis of the British,* failed to meet that challenge. After World War II, Egypt found itself still tied to the cultivation and export of a single crop, cotton. Only timid steps had been taken toward industrialization, but it was increasingly clear that, given Egypt's limited land and high agricultural yields, little more could be expected of agriculture. King Faruq, the last of the Muhammad Ali dynasty, was too distracted by his own pleasures and the intrigues of a venal court to take much interest in economic strategy. Indeed, his last major initiative was typically ill-conceived and ill-prepared. He launched Egypt's poorly equipped army into war against the newly proclaimed state of Israel in May 1948. Egypt's armed forces and the nation itself were humiliated.

This humiliation stimulated a group of young army and air force officers, under Colonel Nasser's leadership, to depose the King and seize

*Great Britain occupied Egypt in 1882, and the last British troops did not quit the country until 1954.

power in July 1952. Their task was essentially four-fold: to rebuild the armed forces to face the Zionist threat; to restructure the economy and promote industrialization; to bring about an equitable distribution of wealth; and to expel the British from the Canal Zone. But Egypt's political arena was by no means a *tabula rasa* at this time. There were several political parties and groups left over from the monarchical period. Most important among these was a quasi-party known as the Society of Muslim Brethren, or the Muslim Brotherhood.

THE MUSLIM BROTHERHOOD

The birth and evolution of this organization is crucial to an understanding of the relation between religion and social change in Egypt. It was founded in 1929 by Hassan al-Banna, a primary school teacher of modest social origins. Through the force of his own personality he began to attract a substantial following. The movement gained momentum during the 1930s when the effects of the world depression made themselves felt in Egypt.

Al-Banna's message stressed a return to the basic precepts of Islam as applied to personal behavior and argued that deviation from these principles had weakened Egyptian society and allowed it to fall under foreign domination. Further, there must be a reassertion of indigenous values and local culture in the face of the corrupting influence of Western ideas. Specifically, the use of Arabic must be undergirded and pseudo-Western cosmopolitanism rooted out of the Egyptian élite. It abhorred the notion of liberal democracy, an imported concept, and argued that in Islam "secular" political authorities must be at the service of the faith. It denounced the multi-party parliamentary system as a sham and condemned the Egyptian politicians who allowed themselves to be manipulated by the British and the King and who believed in the separation of religious and political authority.

The Brotherhood was no more clear about the form an Islamic government would take than is Ayatollah Khomeini in Iran today. But like Khomeini it had a vaguely formulated social program that purported to address the inequitable distribution of wealth and the poverty of the masses. The Brotherhood was the first mass movement to raise these questions, and it had a wide audience as the economic situation deteriorated.

The organization appealed to groups, mainly urban, that had lost status under British control and the impact of Western industrial economies— artisans, small-scale manufacturers, the clergy—and to groups that had been *created* by these forces only to have their upward mobility halted during the depression—petty bureaucrats, school teachers, modern sector labor, etc.

As in Iran 40 years later, the peasants remained relatively aloof although hardly indifferent to this modern assertion of Islam. The archetypal Muslim Brother was probably urban, lower middle class, literate but only in Arabic, politically aware, strongly nationalistic and pious, with very uncertain career perspectives.

That sketch could describe any of a number of the young men in the 1930s who later went on to found the Free Officers movement and to seize power in 1952. Nearly all the top leadership had had more or less intense contacts with the Brotherhood in the 1930s and 1940s. Some abetted it in organizing their paramilitary wing and in training volunteers to harass the British in the Canal Zone and to fight the Zionists in Palestine. Indeed, from 1936 on, the Muslim Brotherhood declared opposition to Zionist settlement in Palestine a holy cause.

When Nasser led the Army to power, four years after the assassination of Hassan al-Banna (presumably by the King's police), the new "Supreme Guide," Hassan Hodeibi, may have thought that the Brotherhood could easily manipulate the young officers. It was a fundamental miscalculation: whatever the ideological affinities between them, Nasser and his colleagues had no intention of allowing the armed forces to become the creature of Hassan Hodeibi. The officers could not tolerate so powerful a political organization when their own institutional underpinnings outside the armed forces were so weak. In 1954, during a public speech, a man in the audience fired at Nasser. After his arrest he claimed the Brotherhood put him up to it. Nasser unleashed his police on the organization and seemingly crushed it.

THE ROAD TO SOCIALISM

From 1954 on, it became clear that Egypt was run by rationalistic, organization men. Many, like Nasser himself and Anwar Sadat, were pious and observant, but they wanted religion to be divorced from state policy. What they shared with the Brotherhood was a fundamental distrust of liberal politics (seen as a game that the rich inevitably dominate and that invites foreign meddling) and of atheistic communism. For all his blustery confrontations with the West and his authoritarian style of rule, Nasser spoke fundamentally in a Western idiom and espoused faith in a managerial-scientific approach to solving Egypt's problems. It was to preempt economic resources from all domestic rivals that Nasser guided his country toward socialism in the late 1950s and early 1960s. The agricultural sector remained in private hands, as did retail, wholesale, and many service trades, but nearly all major industries, banks, insurance, utilities, and foreign trade were put under public ownership.

Egypt entered a phase of self-proclaimed socialist transformation after 1961. This phase was accompanied by increasingly close aid, trade, and military relations with the Soviet Union. The socialization process was not greeted with universal enthusiasm, and even some of Nasser's closest associates abandoned him over it. It did produce undeniable social benefits through increased employment, an expansion of education, and the redistribution of wealth to the poorer strata of society. But it touched still-raw religious nerves that feared a drift toward communism and atheism and the undermining of the principle of private property. Nasser protected himself on that flank by bringing the religious "establishment" under state control: al-Azhar University, the scholarly authoritative voice throughout the Muslim world, was vastly expanded, and its traditionalist core was swamped in an invasion of new disciplines and faculty. The clergy (*ulema*) remained, as they had under the monarchy, relatively docile, and Nasser promoted from their ranks those who endorsed such progressive causes as family planning.

Yet it was at the height of the socialist experiment in 1965 that a new threat from the traditional, conservative religious right became manifest. In August of that year, thousands of suspected members of the outlawed Muslim Brotherhood were rounded up; hundreds were tried for plotting to overthrow the government. The plot was genuine, proving that the Brotherhood had been suppressed but not destroyed. But the most striking aspect of the affair was that those who stood trial were largely from the groups that had most benefited from Nasser's revolution: university students, engineers, civil servants, a smattering of police and army officers, and even an airline pilot. The mastermind of the plot, it was charged, was Sayyid Qutb, an elderly member of the *ulema* who had inveighed in print against Egypt's slide into a new *jahilia*, or age of ignorance, as the period before Islam was known. Qutb's execution in September 1966 provoked a hue and cry throughout the Arab world.

Egypt's humiliating defeat by the Israelis in June 1967 forced Nasser to roll back the socialist experiment on several fronts. One by one his most radical advisors were dropped, and timid steps toward economic liberalization were taken. The level of socialist rhetoric abated. This was a period of turning inward, of searching for inner resources to sustain the country in a period of resistance and "steadfastness" in the face of the Israeli occupation of the Sinai. It was not surprising, in that time of crisis, that the members of the regime turned to Islamic themes and ritual observance for individual solace and collective solidarity. The origins of what has commonly been called the Islamic resurgence lie in that period.

THE RESURGENCE OF ISLAM

To appreciate what has transpired since 1967, several observations are in order. The first has to do with the quality of Egyptian Islam. For most of the 90 percent of the population that claims some degree of adherence to Islam, it is an allegiance worn lightly and unselfconsciously, precisely because the religion has penetrated so deeply. Egypt was Islamized at the beginning of the Islamic era, and Arabic became the standard tongue of the Nile Valley at the same time. In contrast with Muslim societies of very different ethnic and linguistic traditions, Egyptian "Muslimness" is taken for granted as an ineradicable element of national identity. While Egypt is endowed with unquestionably militant Islamic groups, it seems doubtful that strident militancy of the Iranian variety will characterize Egyptian Islam.

That said, it is also the case that the number and activity of Muslim groups have increased since 1967. There are several explanations for this phenomenon, all speculative. Nasser died in September 1970 and was succeeded by his Vice President, Anwar Sadat. Sadat was and is a more conservative man in religious terms than Nasser and a more liberal man in political and economic terms. From the outset he wanted to reduce the influence of the left in Egypt, dismantle the Arab Socialist Union, Egypt's only legal political organization, and stimulate private sector activity in the economy. Bringing about this shift required, so it must have seemed to Sadat, the legitimation of Muslim activity in politics. With little fanfare he gave them the green light. For the first time since 1954, especially in the universities, Muslim fundamentalists began to assert themselves—in student councils, professional syndicates and the Egyptian parliament.

But the genie was out of the bottle. The left was too weak to offer much resistance, and Sadat soon found that he was not in full control of the forces he had let loose. First, there was Qadhafi, Libya's leader since 1969, who preached a kind of militant, leveling Islam. Before the 1973 war, Egypt and Libya planned to establish a unified nation. In preparation for that, Qadhafi was allowed to spread his own interpretation of Islam throughout Egypt. Many were responsive to his appeal, but when he called for a cultural revolution in Egypt, several of his erstwhile Egyptian allies balked

Saudi Arabia was alarmed at the prospect of the virulently antimonarchical Qadhafi using Egypt as a platform to denounce the Saudi regime. Undoubtedly Egypt's major preoccupation was to gain access to some portion of the oil wealth of Libya, and in this respect King Faisal of Saudi Arabia could offer competitve terms. In September 1973, Sadat scrapped his plans for a merger with Lybya and firmed up the "Riyadh-Cairo axis" after the October war.

The new financial weight of Saudi Arabia in Egyptian affairs provided that conservative Muslim regime access to Egypt's religious authorities. Sadat could not thwart the discreet but well-funded efforts of the Saudis to further the return to fundamental Muslim values as long as he needed Saudi money. The principal Egyptian figure in the Saudi camps was Abd Al-Halim Mahmud, the *shaykh* of al-Azhar University and thus a figure of some stature throughout the Muslim world. He was able to lobby successfully for greater freedom for religious groups to function and to publish. He took a strong stand against certain aspects of the emancipation of women, and blocked a liberal revision of Egypt's personal status law.

Sadat was also hindered in containing the ferment on the religious right because, after 1973, he began to pursue cautiously a general policy of political liberalization that led in 1976 to the formation of political parties and the eventual dissolution of the Arab Socialist Union. The laws governing the formation of parties stipulated that none could be founded on the basis of religious or sectarian goals or of class conflict. All parties had to adhere to the principle of national solidarity as embodied in the concept of the "alliance of working forces" and the 1971 Law on National Unity that made illegal, among other things, efforts to sow discord between Coptic Christians and Muslims. It was Sadat's hope that he could build on the center-right to push Muslim fundamentalists, Nasserites, and leftists to the margins of the political arena. In many ways he has succeeded, but the path has been bumpy.

One area of friction since the 1970s has been Coptic-Muslim relations. (According to the Egyptian census of 1976, the Copts make up nearly 7 percent of the population.)

By Middle Eastern standards, however, this friction is not overly acute. Muslims believe that under the British, Copts were favored in the civil service and were overrepresented in the professions. That trend was reversed under Nasser, and the Copts began to complain of discrimination and persecution. Nevertheless, there was little overt conflict between the communities under Nasser. The only major incident occurred in the mid-1960s when the regime claimed to have uncovered a Coptic separatist movement that aimed at establishing a Coptic state in Upper Egypt.

The advent of Sadat in 1970 was soon followed by the election of a new Coptic Patriarch, Baba Shenouda, who became a staunch defender of his community. Because Copts could not easily obtain authorizations to build churches, they resorted to registering private houses or offices as Christian cultural societies and then held religious services in them. Muslims protested this practice, and a series of clashes took place in the town of Khanqa near Cairo in 1972 that led to a parliamentary investigation and a liberalization of rules governing church construction.

Sporadic clashes have continued. Copts were particularly concerned by the momentum behind the Muslim objective of making the *shariah* the source of all law in Egypt. In this spirit a law was introduced in Parliament in 1977 that would have exacted the death penalty for renunciation of Islam. Many Copts who had married Muslims had become nominal Muslims themselves, but it had been accepted that if their spouse died or if they divorced, they could revert to Chistianity. Under the new law, this practice would have become punishable by death. When Shenouda led the Copts in a fast, Sadat had the draft law withdrawn.

Shenouda maintained his militant stance until May 1980, when Sadat publicly accused him of trying to erect a state within the state. Sadat went on to declare the principle of "no politics in religion; no religion in politics." His condemnation was of the Coptic leadership, but his message was to Muslim fundamentalists. Police surveillance of all forms of religious activity was stepped up.

Muslim activities in the mid-1970s accelerated appreciably, but the movements were highly factionalized. The Muslim Brotherhood had reemerged legally and was allowed its own publications. Its message touched particularly on foreign policy, and it openly denounced the Camp David accords. The organization also opposed further emancipation of women, argued for various measures of sexual segregation, and opposed legislation that gave women the right to initiate divorce. Muslim student groups simultaneously gained control of student councils in most universities under a coalition, the "Islamic Association." Operating covertly were splinter groups ranging from self-proclaimed Muslim Marxists to the Repentence and Holy Flight Group.

The latter grouping, mainly young, fairly well-educated Egyptians of provincial origins and both sexes, had withdrawn from what they regarded as a corrupt society. They considered reform an illusion and opted instead for assault. In an earlier organizational incarnation they tried to engineer a coup d'etat by enlisting the support of cadets in the military academy (April 1974). Then, in July 1977, they kidnapped the Minister of Religious Endowments and demanded the release of those arrested in 1974. When their demands went unmet, they killed the Minister. Many more were arrested, and their leader eventually was executed.

Khomeini's successful movement in Iran lent hope to these groups in Egypt. But Sadat is not the Shah, nor is Egypt socially or economically like Iran. Sadat does not run a police state, and he has not emasculated his own middle class. However conservative and pious his entourage and political class, they do not want an Islamic state. And however impatient Sadat may become with his establishment critics, as embodied in the legal opposition the

"Socialist Labor Party" led by Ibrahim Shukry, the moderate middle is not going to abdicate to Sadat's whim or wilt in the face of Islamic fervor.

For his part, Sadat has had to wage a complicated battle to maintain a semblance of liberal politics without jeopardizing his political control. Islamic fundamentalists are only one player in this game. Because their banner is religion they are hard to silence or repress unless the regime is willing to return to Nasser's police methods. But even then, given Egypt's present mood, repression might merely serve to create martyrs and perhaps produce the charismatic leadership that has been lacking. Sadat's strategy had been to secure the allegiance of the authorities of al-Azhar, while underscoring that institution's role as judge and monitor of correct belief and conduct for orthodox Muslims. In other words, Sadat wants to use his own religious supporters to isolate his Muslim critics. There is one issue, however, about which he can expect little more than discreet silence from al-Azhar, and that is his policy toward peace with Israel. Sadat has been unable to achieve a consensus among Muslim groups about the wisdom of his course.

As the Reagan administration settles in, Egypt finds itself marking time in its efforts to promote the peace process with Israel. In the absence of progress on that front, President Sadat has resisted the implementation of economic reforms—such as ending direct and indirect subsidies of consumer goods—that would lead to greater efficiency but also to economic hardship especially for the urban poor and those on low, fixed incomes. For the moment Egypt has the financial resources, fueled by remittances of Egyptians working abroad and by earnings from the sale of petroleum, to pay for these policies. But they have been accompanied by high rates of inflation, the presence of a growing foreign business community, and by an ostentatious class of Egyptian entrepreneurs who have made fortunes in urban real estate speculation and the importation of vast amounts of luxury consumer goods. When these elements are coupled with widespread corruption at all levels, and Egypt's increasingly close military ties with the United States, it is not difficult to see the makings of a situation that could threaten the Sadat government. It is the kind of situation that profoundly disturbs many Egyptians, and the various Islamic groups have appealing, if simplistic, remedies to offer.

5

Pakistan, Islam, and the Politics of Muslim Unrest

Mowahid H. Shah

*A*BOUT THE SIZE OF TEXAS AND LOUISIANA COMBINED, Pakistan, a land of 80 million, is a key country in the Islamic commonwealth. Sharing borders with India, China, Iran, and now Soviet-occupied Afghanistan, Pakistan has shown remarkable capacity to maintain cordial ties with the diverse Muslim nations of the Middle East, such as Turkey, Iran, and most of the Arab world. Though not oil-rich, its potential for leadership has been amply demonstrated by the successive hosting of two Islamic conferences in the recent past. Additionally, the influx of over a million Afghan refugees, and the presence of the headquarters of Afghan resistance groups in Peshawar, assures that Pakistan will play a major role in attempts to resolve the question of the Soviet occupation of Afghanistan. Described as a "backdoor" to the Persian Gulf, Pakistan is also of important strategic concern to the West.

Formed from British India in 1947, Pakistan is unique among modern states in that it is the only state to have been founded on the basis of Muslim nationhood. The stated aim behind the idea of Pakistan, as propounded by the philosopher-poet Iqbal and subsequently executed by Mohammed Ali Jinnah, was to carve out the Muslim majority areas from British India in order to form an independent state for the Muslims. Pakistan, therefore, was meant to be a country of Muslims banded together for common purposes, central among which was a desire to be separate and free from Hindu domination in undivided India.

In his quest, Jinnah, the creator of Pakistan, was vigorously opposed by the organized Muslim clergy, who felt that the universality of Islam would be limited by its territorial confinement within a modern nation-state. Jinnah was clear in his concept of a sovereign homeland for the Muslims. But he also made it clear that Pakistan should not be structured along the traditional orthodox lines advocated by his conservative/religious opponents. Stated in his own words, "Pakistan would not be a 'theocratic state' ruled by 'priests.'"

 Ironically, the dominant ideology of the present government is of those religious groups which opposed Jinnah and the concept of Pakistan. This paradox forms one of Pakistan's major dilemmas in charting its future course.

Should the West then consider the current "Islamization" in Pakistan as part of the worldwide Islamic fervor? Superficially, the answer seems to be in the affirmative, but a closer examination indicates the reasons have more to do with internal politics. In particular, Pakistan reflects a heightened official recognition of the effectiveness of Islam as an instrument to retain governmental control—especially so for a regime with a narrow political base.

In power since July 1977, when it ousted Prime Minister Zulfikar Ali Bhutto in a coup d'etat, the Zia government announced itself as a caretaker administration which would stay on only until fair and free elections could be held. Yet, a short time later, it introduced substantive changes in the country's political structure. Elections were rescheduled on numerous occasions, but have not taken place because "un-Islamic forces should not be permitted to participate." Although Zia, in April 1977, had equated oppostion to the autocratic Bhutto as treason, he toppled Bhutto three months later. After a trial which attempted, among other things, to demonstrate that Bhutto was not a good Muslim, Zia eventually had him hanged.

Despite an earlier government statement that elections were necessary because prolonging military rule would spell disaster for Pakistan, elections are now condemned as a Western aberration unsuited to Pakistan's polity. With some justification, Pakistanis view these governmental attempts to stagemanage Islam as motivated more by considerations of self-preservation than by genuine conviction in favor of an Islamic order.

Pakistan has, is, and seems likely to be plagued by poor leadership. The pattern of blurring the distinction between government and state is continuing. Sucessive governments have presented themselves as entities synonymous with the state and thus have equated opposition with treason, calling opponents "anti-state elements." An elaboration of this theme will be an attempt to attribute opposition to Zia's "Islamic government" as heresy emanating from anti-Islamic elements.

Pakistan is overwhelmingly Muslim, and its masses feel a deep indentification with Islam. Why, then, has Zia's "Islamic government" not been greeted with an outburst of popular enthusiasm? The issue is one of credibility. The masses feel that religion should be a matter of voluntary practice and not policed as a mandatory observance. In the same way, the religious parties have traditionally fared poorly at the polls. Official Islam is one thing and popular Islam something else. Official Islam is a tactic to impede access to social justice, while the popular conception of Islam is that of a code of life in which social justice is at the center of human endeavor. Hence, when the Muslims speak of Islam, it is another way of asking for the dismantling of an unjust social order. Their goal is not that the visible duties of Islam, such as prayers and fasting, be rigorously enforced by the state. What they wish is that opportunity for a better life should not be a privilege of the elite but a common expectation for all. Indeed, state-enforced Islam, unaccompanied by fundamental socioeconomic uplift, may well lead to a massive blacklash against religious regimentation.

In fact, Muslim unrest in Pakistan and elsewhere has surfaced for reasons more political than religious. The major cause of the general Islamic upheaval is a total disenchantment with the corruption of the governing élites, around which is the aura of concentrated wealth, power, and all the benefits of twentieth-century Western technology. The élites are perceived as parasitical, insensitive, and hypocritical. Their sanctimonious public rhetoric is contrasted with their private conduct, which often is an eloquent rebuttal to what they publicly profess.

This is the establishment which the West—obsessed with the status quo and "stability"—assiduously courts. But while the West views stability as vital to its security interests and thus to be maintained at all costs, the Muslim masses see it as the path to a tomorrow which is merely a rerun of bleak yesterdays. Even that citadel of "stability," Dr. Henry Kissinger, has acknowledged belatedly that "in an era of revolutionary change, it is a mistake to rely on a reactionary status quo."

In countries where freedom of assembly and political expression is restricted and where alternative means to ventilate grievances may be absent, the mosque provides a forum to congregate and articulate common concerns. Such was the case in Iran. But Pakistan is not Iran. In Iran, Islam was used by the people to topple a militaristic order whereas in Pakistan it is used by the martial law government against the people to insure maintenance of its power. Moreover, while nearly all Iranians are shii Muslims sharing common religious orientation, the monolithic sunni orthodoxy of General Zia alienates many of Pakistan's sizeable shii minority and also substantial elements among the sunnis themselves.

In the context of the worldwide Islamic resurgence, Zia's objectives are threefold: (1) to draw support from the Muslim world; (2) to ingratiate himself with the conservative orthodoxy of Saudi Arabia (Pakistan's principal financial backer); and (3) to show a nexus with the Iranian revolution and add legitimacy to his rule (although during the movement against the Shah, Zia viewed the Shah's ouster as a threat to the stability of Pakistan).

But, if Pakistan is not analogous to Iran, what led to the burning of the U.S. Embassy in Islamabad in 1979? Although the manifestation of that unfortunate action was religious, the reasons behind it were political, based on a long-smoldering resentment against the United States.

When the Pakistan government rejected the Carter Administration's offer of $400 million in economic and military assistance—a step General Zia took to broaden his political base at home and abroad—it also happened to comport with a deep-seated Pakistani disenchantment with the quality of American friendship. The feeling in Pakistan has been that the United States for too long has taken Pakistan's friendship for granted, a perception based on experience with the United States over nearly three decades.

Apprehensive of India, Pakistan in the mid-1950s sought security through formal alignment. Then, as now, the establishment placed more emphasis on external props than on developing enduring institutions. In fact, one Pakistani President viewed America as an "eternal friend" allied with Pakistan out of altruistic concerns. Thus, when Pakistan chose an alliance, it was not with neighboring China or the Soviet Union but with the United States, nearly 10,000 miles away. As an offshoot of its new bond, Pakistan also "adopted" two enemies among its neighbors, i.e., China and the USSR. Subsequent events have tested the wisdom of this alliance.

In the West, India—which spurned close ties with the United States—has been portrayed in a more favorable light than Pakistan. Although India has annexed Kashmir, Junagadh, Hyderabad, Goa, and Sikkim, it still is romanticized in many Western nations as the peace-loving moral conscience of the Third World, while Pakistan is often judged negatively.

Pakistanis also point out that while India for years has been friendly to Soviet interests and has shown contempt for U.S. policies, it has been rewarded with substantial military, economic, food, and nuclear assistance from the United States. In 1965, when Indian armies marched to within shouting distance of Pakistan's historic city of Lahore, the United States—the principal source of armaments for Pakistan—chose at that crucial moment to cut off the supply of weapons, whereas China, in striking contrast, offered to intervene militarily on Pakistan's behalf. Earlier, in 1962, when non-aligned India fought against China, U.S. military aid was pumped into India—without consultation with Pakistan—despite later Pakistani protestations that one day the same arms might be directed against Pakistan.

Nine years later, in 1971, when India, with Soviet approval, was in the process of dismembering Pakistan, no tangible U.S. assistance was offered, notwithstanding the celebrated "tilt."

Pakistanis also remember the year 1960 when Francis Gary Powers took off from the U.S. communications base in Peshawar on his ill-fated U-2 spy flight over the Soviet Union. For its role, Pakistan was threatened with annihilation by Khrushchev. It is also recalled—and later was acknowledged by Nixon and Kissinger—how Pakistan, by acting as a bridge between Peking and Washington, paved the way for one of America's greatest foreign policy accomplishments since World War II.

Pakistanis feel that, over the years, the United States has not been a reliable ally, and that American aid has not been given when needed most, leaving Pakistan in the lurch and forcing it to seek friendship with China. To many Pakistanis, the same scenario seems capable of repetition, especially in the wake of the Russian takeover in Afghanistan.

The climate of distrust is such that some Pakistanis believe that the United States was behind the removal of Bhutto in July 1977 and that America could, if it had wanted to, have forestalled the execution of the flamboyant ex-Premier. This is coupled with popular resentment against U.S. opposition to Pakistan's nuclear program which was inflamed further by Carter's attempt to ship enriched uranium to India, a move seen as another example of U.S. inconsistency and double-dealing.

Until recently, Pakistan—primarily because of its pro-American posture—was never totally accepted in the Third World, and repeated attempts to join the nonaligned movement met with failure. In 1979 in Havana Pakistan was for the first time permitted to participate. Much more than $400 million in U.S. aid and a vague commitment to come to Pakistan's defense would have been needed to induce Pakistan to leave the nonaligned camp.

In the experience of Pakistan and other Third World countries, the benefits of maintaining friendship with the United States are far outweighed by its political burdens, and such a friendship, even if buttressed by "iron-clad" commitments, becomes meaningless when subject to the capriciousness of U.S. domestic politics.

What should the United States do? One indispensable step in removing the growing cancer in Islamic-Western ties would be to fashion a solution to the Arab-Israeli dispute that meets Palestinian aspirations for self-determination and statehood. Not to do so would be to continue White House irresponsibility in playing politics with a problem whose unresolved status threatens to pit the West against the Islamic world. Also, it weakens the credibility of the professed American empathy toward the Afghan resistance to the Soviet presence.

The other step would be to understand the basis of Islamic populism on a country-to-country basis by keeping the lines of communication open with the people and by not underrating the power of Muslim solidarity. With respect to Pakistan, America should uphold the territorial integrity of Pakistan without identifying itself with the Zia regime—a policy which China has successfully demonstrated.

A popular misconception fed to Westerners in part by conservative Muslim rulers attributes the Muslim upheaval to a "too rapid modernization" which has brought about a clash between modernity and the well-entrenched traditions that the people are loath to discard. Undoubtedly, the Muslim world has many honorable traditions which it wishes to preserve. But alongside these are other unfortunate traditions: poverty, illiteracy, disease, treating women like prisoners of war, glaring economic inequality, absence of social justice. How many people would wish to protect these traditions from the "disruptive change" wrought by modernity. In fact, given the opportunity, the *mustazafin*—the ones bypassed by society—would not hesitate to become the *mustakbarin*—the possessors of the benefits of modernity.

So long as the methods for implementing social change are well thought out, it is difficult to visualize the majority poor rising up in revolt because their governments committed the mistake of trying to better their lives by making health care, education, and other participatory opportunities accessible to them.

Islam began as a revolution against ignorance. Yet, today—1400 years from its founding—the freshness of the youngest world faith is debilitated by mass ignorance. The fault lies not with the disenfranchised Muslim masses but with their dishonest leaders whose interests are served and strengthened by keeping the people as ill-informed as possible. Mass illiteracy guarantees that Islam will be used more to impede progress and less to aid it. So long as this pattern continues, the potential of the Muslim world cannot be translated into effective political power.

It has been said, with substantial justification, that Islam is not adequately understood in the West. But as before, Islam will be judged in the fourth quarter of the twentieth century more by the conduct of its followers than by its humane precepts. The challenge Muslims face, therefore, is to realize the Holy Prophet's revolutionary message by identifying Islam as an ally of progress instead of its foe. In that realization could be the beginnings of a true Islamic renaissance.

6

Education and Family Life in Modernizing Malaysia

Muhammad Kamal bin Hassan

$\mathcal{M}$ ALAYSIA, WITH A POPULATION OF APPROXIMATELY 12.5 MILLION, is one of the few Asian countries which has attained a relatively high standard of living. Its per capita income—US$500 in 1970—is the third highest in Asia, after Japan and Singapore. Economic and political achievements notwithstanding, Malaysia has been grappling with a host of internal problems peculiar to a multiracial country* and a secular state in which Islam is the official religion and in which the Malays, who are the adherents of Islam, form the bulk of the economically poor.

One of the major problems of post-1969 Malaysia is the question of raising the economic status of the Malays in the rural as well as the urban sectors, so that by the year 1990 the Bumiputera (i.e., the Malays as well as other indigenous peoples of Malaysia) will have achieved a 30 percent equity in the modern corporate sector of an open-market economy traditionally dominated by the Chinese and by foreign concerns. This is the main objective of the New Economic Policy incorporated in the Second Malaysia Plan (1971–1975), the Third Malaysia Plan (1976–1980), and the forthcoming Fourth Malaysia Plan (1981–1985). The impact of this national policy of raising the living standards of the rural poor and transforming, as it were, the Malay into an industrialized *gesellschaft* with an entrepreneurial and

---

*The *1981 World Factbook* lists the population of Malaysia as composed of 50 percent Malay, 35 percent Chinese, 10 percent persons from the South Asian subcontinent, and 5 percent others.

managerial class of its own, upon the development of Islam and Muslims in Malaysia, is indeed a fascinating subject for all students of development and religion in the Third World.

An essentially growth-oriented program of development in Malaysia based upon a diffusionist model of development implies a considerable degree of secularization of culture and society. As such, the manner in which Malaysian Muslims respond to the processes of secularization in economic development, education, law, culture, and politics is indicative of the force of Islam and of the unresolved conflicts within the Muslim community. The issue between tradition and change in the Malaysian context, then, does not arise out of "modernization versus Islam" but out of a particular type of approach to development coming into contact with a particular type of Muslim religiosity and consciousness which ranges from the secularist, the accommodationist, to the wholistic or from the legitimizing, the permissive, to the puritanist. The scope of the encounter is too large to be treated in this essay, which will focus on two areas of Muslim life affected by the process of modernization in the form of the national development programs: education and family.

EDUCATION

It is stated in the Rukunegara (the official ideology of the state) that Malaysia is dedicated "to achieving a greater unity for all her peoples; to maintaining a democratic way of life; to creating a just society in which the wealth of the nation shall be equitably distributed; to ensuring a liberal approach to her rich and diverse cultural traditions; to building a progressive society which shall be oriented to modern science and technology." The way to achieve these goals is by following the five principles: "Belief in God; Loyalty to King and Country; Upholding the Constitution; Rule of Law; Good Behavior and Morality." In accordance with these objectives of national integration, building a science and technology-oriented society and redressing economic imbalances—particularly between the Malays and the Chinese—education in Malaysia becomes a major instrument of socioeconomic and cultural change.

The Mid-Term Review of the Second Malaysia Plan, 1971–1975, observes that there has been a significant expansion of educational programs to enable a greater number of Malays and other Bumiputera to meet the requirements of racially balanced employment and a viable Malay commercial and industrial community. Expansion of facilities and opportunities for education in science, mathematics, and technology-oriented disciplines also took place. One of the major thrusts of the Third Malaysia Plan (1976–1980) is that education and training systems are geared to equip youth with the knowledge and skills necessary for their effective participation in developing the economy. For this purpose the teaching of science and mathematics at primary and lower secondary levels is strengthened; science, technical and vocational courses in upper secondary education are also expanded. In tertiary education, the intake of liberal arts students is progressively reduced and priority is given to diploma-level courses to meet the sizeable demand for manpower at the subprofessional level. Meanwhile, continuing efforts are being made to increase enrollments of Malay students in local and foreign universities to bring about a balance that accords with the long-term objective of restructuring the ethnic composition of employment in professional, technical, and managerial occupations.

The bias for science and technical education presumably will continue to be a significant feature of Malaysia's educational policy for a long time to come, considering the recent realization among Malay political and intellectual élites that, after ten years of the implementation of the New Economic Policy since 1971, the achievement of Malays in the economy has been dismally low: they have only acquired ten percent ownership of the economy. It was also revealed in the Third Bumiputera Economic Congress in Kuala Lumpur in May 1980, that "since independence till this day, we [the Malays] have only 527 engineers compared to 4,572 non-Malays, 218 doctors compared to 2,840 non-Malays and 45 architects compared to 457 non-Malays." It was disclosed that in the University of Malaya—the biggest and oldest university in the country—out of 253 students who graduated in engineering in 1979, only 79 were Malays, 31.2 percent of the total. In the case of medical students, only 68, or 42 percent, of the 162 graduating doctors were Bumiputera. In the science faculty 378 or 40.9 percent of the 925 graduates were Bumiputera. The Vice Chancellor of the University of Malaya was quoted as saying recently that Bumiputeras only achieve 10 percent of the total number of graduates who obtained first class and second class (upper) honors degree, whereas at the lower levels of the bachelor's degree, almost three quarters of the graduates were Bumiputeras.

The leaders of Islamic opinion in the country generally support the idea of having more Muslim technocrats, doctors, and other professionals. If they have voiced any concern, it was directed not against science education or technology-oriented education as such. It was the divorce of education and training, at home and abroad, from Islamic moral and spiritual values which drew the criticism from Islamic quarters. The serious criticisms did not originate from the *ulema* presumably because of their lack of access to knowledge regarding the state of modern sciences and the intellectual and cultural challenges currently facing Muslim students in British or American universities. It is not surprising, therefore, that the voices of concern regarding the independence of scientific and professional disciplines from moral and spiritual values came largely from the Malay-educated élites who were the products of secular English education, either during the colonial period or after independence in 1957.

While Professor Syed Muhammad al-Naquib al-Attas is the principal exponent of the philosophical-metaphysical approach to educational issues in Malaysia—his major contribution being the exposition of the Islamic theory of knowledge—a more typical, down-to-earth criticism of contemporary secular education in Malaysia may be seen in Dr. Nik Abdul Rashid's essay entitled "Islamic Education Checks Value Crisis and Moral Decadence." A professor of Western law, Nik Abdul Rashid sees the rising incidence of urban crime, prostitution, gambling, corruption, misuse of power, and other aspects of moral decadence in urban Malaysia as manifestations of a crisis of values created by a development strategy aimed largely at economic growth and material prosperity. Technical education and professional training which ignore moral and spiritual values also contribute to the decline of ethical standards in Malaysia's cities. "Only through Islamic education," he said, "could moral decay be checked if not entirely eradicated." Other critics have also suggested a correlation between corruption, bribery, abuse of power, and mismanagement in governmental and financial institutions involving Malay technocrats, bankers, managers and political leaders, and the lack of ethical content in the educational background of those élites.

It would be incorrect to suggest that the government has completely ignored Islamic education in the national system of education. Since independence in 1957, Islamic religious knowledge constitutes a part of the curriculum (i.e., 120 minutes per school week) for Muslim pupils of secondary schools wherever there are 15 or more Muslims in a class. But since it is not necessary to pass school examinations in Islamic knowledge, it has not received serious attention by the pupils. However, with the creation of the Division of Religious Education in the Ministry of Education in 1975, many important steps were taken to strengthen Islamic education in the country. The Ministry has recently announced that by 1983, moral values will be taught as a school subject to be taken by all non-Muslim pupils, while Islamic knowledge is being given to the Muslim pupils. A new subject, Arabic, will be introduced in all secondary schools in the near future. Prayer halls for Muslim pupils have already become a familiar feature of secondary government schools in Malaysia. The Ministry also allows Muslim girls to wear the headcover and long dress to school, which formerly was the practice of only the pupils of the religious schools (*madrasahs*). The curriculum of the religious schools administered by the Ministry has also been changed to accommodate more non-religious subjects.

The MARA Institute of Technology too offers a three-year course on Islamic civilization, while the five universities in the country provide courses on Islam. However, only two universities make it obligatory for all students to take special courses on Islam at the undergraduate level. In the universities it is not uncommon to see female Muslim students in the science, medical, or social science faculties wearing the traditional Islamic headcover, which has now become one of the visible indicators of Islamic consciousness. It has been observed that the consciousness of Islamic identity tends to be stronger among science and technical students than among the social science students, both at home and abroad. One discerns a yearning among the younger generation of educated Muslims today for inner contentment and self-identity. Many of them are seeking direction in the moral and spiritual development of their personality which, through education, seems to be caught between new cultural forces operating in urban society in the form of permissive lifestyles, utilitarian individualism, and the ostentatious living of the nouveau riche, on the one hand, and on the other, a religious vision of emotional stability, moderation in consumption, concern for the underprivileged and undernourished masses, a reenactment of the timeless value of moral rectitude in the face of crass and shameless materialism, and an idealistic environment.

Without this insight into the psychospiritual orientation of the present-day Muslim intelligentsia who are witnessing the grave consequences of the process of secularization in national development efforts, it would be difficult to explain fully the case of a group of university graduates deciding to leave their professions and lucrative jobs in Kuala Lumpur in favor of migrating to a rural area and establishing a sufi-type religious commune. Similarly, it would take more than employing the structural opposition concept of some social scientists to try to understand the case of several university students in the natural sciences and in the humanities joining a large "fundamentalist" religious community known as Dar-al-Arqam on the outskirts of the city of Kuala Lumpur. This community aims at self-sufficiency and self-reliance in its economic activities and runs a clinic and a school system of its own to provide the kind of education that it perceives as most relevant to the needs of society.

This revival of Muslim educational tradition, though on a small scale, is significant because another traditional religious educational system common to both Malaysia and Indonesia, namely the *pondok* (or *pesantren* in Java) system has become a dying institution. This once-flourishing, rural-based and privately owned voluntary educational institution centering around the personality of the *alim* (religious scholar) is indeed an endangered indigenous educational system. This has happened because it has not been able to adjust itself—in terms of curriculum development, organization, and physical growth—to the needs of rural development, rural-urban migration, the winds of political change, and the expansion of the modern religious schools and colleges. Many Muslim leaders and educators express regret at the loss of a vigorous religious education which was generally pursued not because of its economic worth, but for the sake of knowledge and piety.

On the question of the Muslim family in the context of modernization, I shall focus on three areas of contemporary interest: 1) the position of the Malay urban squatter families in and around Kuala Lumpur: 2) the issue of the poor Malay village girls who migrated to the city to work as factory workers; and 3) reforms of the administration of Muslim personal law.

As a result of socioeconomic, historical and political factors, the most important being the "pull" factor of rapid industrialization in the urban areas which had to depend on abundant cheap labor to sustain the new growth centers, and the "push" factor in the increase of landless peasants, rural unemployment and rural poverty in general, Kuala Lumpur and its outskirts have the highest number of squatter families in the country. About one-quarter of the population of the Federal Territory in which Kuala Lumpur is situated is made up of squatters, many of whom are poor Malays who migrated from the villages to work as manual laborers, factory workers, officeboys, washer women, bus drivers, gardeners, etc. Living in illegal squatter settlements and slums in the city, these rural-urban migrants and their problems accentuate the "culture of poverty" as one of the consequences of unbalanced development which gives priority to industrialization.

The Muslim family entangled in this culture of urban poverty lives in constant fear of the antisocial elements that are involved in crimes and other forms of deviant behavior, such as drug abuse, robbery and extortion, rape, sexual promiscuity, and prostitution. According to the Deputy Prime Minister, there are approximately 360,000 drug addicts in the country. Of those seeking medical treatment for drug addiction in the state of Johor in 1976, for example, 72.2 percent were Malays, 21.5 percent Chinese and 6.3 percent Indians. Drug abuse in the Malay family is not confined to the lower-income groups; it is also found among upper middle-class Malays as well.

As far as changes in the function of the family are concerned, there are studies to show that with the increasing trend toward the nuclear family among Malay urban squatters, the family as an economic cooperative unit is declining because the children of marriageable age are expected to find their own means of subsistence, thus contributing to the increase of neolocal families. Although the type of extended family peculiar to some traditional rural communities is relatively rare in the squatter settlements owing to various economic and spatial constraints, it should not be assumed that traditional bonds of the rural-urban migrant with the larger kinship group in the village are giving way under the impact of creeping individualism, urbanization, and the highly competitive market economy of the city. In the case of the lower-income group of Malays living in the urban slums, the physical separation of the individual from his rural environment is not to be mistaken for the breaking of familial ties. Many of the Malay migrants who leave their spouses and children behind in the villages send back monthly remittances to maintain the family and to buy property in the rural areas. In spite of the physical distance, family ties are still strong among the Malays as a whole, more so in the case of the poor Malays.

There has been increasing concern, however, about the generation gap in the well-to-do sections of the Malay community, but the influence of religious values transmitted through informal educational channels, such as the regular Koran reading classes, Sunday religious lectures at the nearby mosque and the greater visibility of religious awareness in the city, helps somewhat in keeping the family together, and the influence of Islamic values and norms regarding the relationship between the young and the old in the Malaysian context cannot be underestimated.

It has also been shown that among the squatters, there is a greater tendency to observe certain Malay customs related to village life if those customs possess religious significance, such as the practice of circumcision, marriage ceremonies, *Isra* and *Miraj* (ascension of the Prophet) celebrations and Maulud Nabi (birthday of the Prophet).

The case of the female Malay factory workers in the city also deserves attention because it is related to the situation of the squatter families in the tension between traditional values and urbanizing lifestyles. Like their male counterparts, these village girls who come to live and work in the industrial areas are exposed for the first time to the insecurities of highly congested living conditions in the slums, away from the congenial atmosphere of their original homes in the village. They have not been conditioned or adequately equipped, educationally or economically, to face the prospects of living by themselves for a long period of extended adolescence forced upon them by the need to support the larger family back in the village. Under the circumstances, relations with the other sex tend to be liberal, for one reason or the other, in some groups, and this has led to rumors about the alleged laxity of sexual behavior among the "factory girls."

The religious authorities have become alarmed at the reports of *khalwat* (close proximity between an unmarried couple) cases among them, and steps are being taken to prevent the recurrence of such deviant sexual behavior by organizing religious classes, and prayer meetings, as well as sending anti-vice officers to apprehend overly promiscuous couples. The religious authorities in the state of Selangor, which is the center of industrial growth in Malaysia, have also approached various factory managers to ask them to allow the Malay workers to be given permission to attend the Friday congregational prayers and to have prayer facilities on the factory premises, so that the Muslim workers, male and female, could perform their prayers at the prescribed times of the day. The results of the negotiations have not been very fruitful.

Meanwhile, the press reports an increase in *khalwat* cases in the states in Selangor, Melaka, and Johor. The director of Selangor's religious department attributed the increasing incidence of *khalwat*, among other causes, to the congested living conditions of the squatters, the lack of decent accommodations and the living together of bachelor men and women resulting from such straitened circumstances. As a solution he suggested that the employers of these factory workers provide proper housing for the migrant workers, along with such facilities as running water, electricity, and modern sanitation. "If these workers were given proper accommodation by their respective employers," said the director, "not only could there be greater control of their sexual behavior, but religious teaching and preaching could be better organized for them."

The state which has the highest number of divorces in Malaysia is Kelantan, which is one of the least economically developed states. Although the number of divorces from 1948 to 1977 has been steadily declining, (11,625 in 1948 to 4,279 in 1977 compared to Selangor's 1,017 in 1970 to 811 in 1975), it is still considered very high. According to the Chief *Qadi* (judge) of Kelantan, financial problems are the main causes of divorce in that state. It is well known in Malaysia that Kelantan has the highest number of male migrants of peasant origins seeking blue-collar jobs in Singapore and Kuala Lumpur. The income they obtain in the cities is not always sufficient to support their families left in Kelantan. "Sometimes for months and years, the wives did not receive money from the husbands who had joined the ranks of the urban squatters. In the end the wives filed a complaint to the Islamic Shariah Court and divorce was obtained," explained the judge of the Court.

Another factor which contributes to Kelantan's high rate of divorce is the weakness in enforcing Islamic law. Besides, some of the officials who are entitled to register marriages and divorces derive their income from the commission deducted from the registration fees. The administration of Islamic personal law is not uniform in all the states, since each state has its own religious bureaucracy which regulates the administration of Islamic law in its own way.

Selangor's administration of Islamic personal law appears to be more efficient and more responsive to the demands for reform than that of most other states for a number of reasons. First, it has a very able director who is oriented to solving problems. Second, being the most advanced state in Malaysia (and the site of the capital), Selangor's administration is constantly exposed to the opinions and criticism of the country's élites. Third, the

Muslim women's organizations in Selangor have a long record of showing great interest in the welfare of Muslim women. As a result of constant prodding from these feminist pressure groups, Selangor has come up with new ideas aimed at improving the administration of Islamic law and giving the female members of the Muslim community the kind of just treatment they deserve from those who administer God's law.

The steps taken by Selangor's Department of Religious Affairs have been lauded by the Minister of Public Welfare, who is herself a fighter for better treatment of Muslim women in the country. Thanks to the untiring efforts of the leaders of the women's movement in the country, including the above-mentioned Minister, a Draft Administration of Muslim Personal Law has been completed. If passed by Parliament, it will be the first attempt at standardizing the administration of Muslim family law in the country.

CONCLUSION

With the increasing consciousness of the relevance of Islam to all aspects of national life, one can expect stronger pressure in the future for a greater accommodation between Islamic values and Malaysian society and culture. Liberal and manpower education, as well as secularizing urbanization, would have to come to terms with the constant Muslim demand for the infusion of Islamic moral values in the process of economic, political, and sociocultural changes. There is, therefore, an urgent need for the government and the Muslim pressure groups to start communicating with each other so that both parties can understand and appreciate their respective positions.

The plight of the Muslim family and the education of the future generation are matters of serious concern to the morally conscious Malays in the government and to the Muslim community. The preservation of Islamic values ought to be maintained by both parties without incurring the sacrifice of the beneficial aspects of development. This balance between stability and change can only be sustained if the government and the Islamic groups can both express their concerns objectively, i.e., without being motivated primarily by selfish political party sentiments.

7

Bangladesh

COMPOSITE CULTURAL IDENTITY AND MODERNIZATION IN A MUSLIM-MAJORITY STATE

Peter J. Bertocci

*A*LTHOUGH NO BIGGER IN AREA THAN THE STATE OF WISCONSIN, Bangladesh is in population the second largest Muslim-majority nation-state in the world today. Seventy million of its 83 million people are Muslims and, after Indonesia, only India and Pakistan rival Bangladesh in the sheer numbers of their citizens who espouse the Muslim faith. Bengalis represent the second largest ethnolinguistic group, after the Arabs, in which Islam predominates. In addition to the Bengali Muslims of Bangladesh, upwards of 13 million others are variously found in several of the Indian states and in Burma.

Islam came to the Bengal region of the Indian subcontinent at the end of the thirteenth century, in the wake of a succession of Muslim ruling powers in the area, the culmination of which was Moghul rule from 1526 to 1757. The efforts of sufi saints, rather than military conquest, are credited with the rapid and widespread conversion of Bengalis to Islam during the early period of Muslim contact. At that time most Bengalis were at least nominally Hindu, or else, even at that late date, Buddhists, but it seems that the mystical and social egalitarian appeal of sufi Islam struck a deeply responsive chord among them. Although it has ben argued that Islam in Bengal is heavily sufi in interpretation, most Bengalis today are sunni Muslims who follow the Hanafi school of Islamic law. The orthodox practices associated with the "five pillars of Islam" are widely observed in Bangladesh. The daily individual and weekly congregational prayer requirements are regularly fulfilled, the month

of fasting (*Ramadan*) is faithfully undergone by most Muslims and the
pilgrimage to Mecca (*hajj*) is undertaken by many who can afford it. All the
Muslim feast and ceremonial days are celebrated, with prominence expect-
ably given to *Id ul-Fitr* (which breaks the fast at the end of Ramadan) and *Id
ul-Azha* (commemorating Abraham's sacrifice). Moreover, it is interesting, if
surprising, that among the sunni Muslims of Bengal the mourning ceremonial
the tenth day of the month of *Muharram* (which commemorates the
martyrdom of Ali's son Hussein) is observed, its ritual activities and
paraphernalia reflecting an historical affinity with shiism. Clearly, then, Islam
has sunk deep roots in Bengali soil.

But Bengali Muslims also share, along with Hindus and far smaller
numbers of Buddhists and Christians, a diverse complex of cultural and social
patterns which are distinctly Indic, most saliently marked by common usage
of the Bengali language and inheritance of its literary traditions. Even after
the coming of Islam there long existed a common Bengali culture which
militated against the warring distinctions of custom which Hindu and Muslim
élites sought to impose. Well into the nineteenth century there persisted a
syncretism in the popular Bengali practice of both Hinduism and Islam, noted
for emotive and substantive similarities even at points where formal
theological and metaphysical doctrines otherwise greatly differed. Indeed, it
might well be argued that the generalized sunni orthodoxy pervading Bengali
Islam today owes itself in goodly measure to the success of powerful Islamic
revivalist movements which reached Bengal from western Asia and swept
across it only in the last century. Thus, Bengali Muslims are the bearers of
what may be seen as a composite cultural identity, uniting both "Muslimness" and "Bengaliness." Their adherence to Islam is readily apparent to the
most casual present-day observer. But at the same time pride of language,
including a distinguished literary tradition, as well as commonality with
non-Muslims in a diversity of social customs and modes of thought, combine
in a distinctive Bengali ethnicity. It is the interaction between these two foci of
cultural identity which, under Western impact and modernization, has shaped
Bangladeshi nationalism over nearly two centuries, finally produced the
national state of Bangladesh itself, and continues to mold the Bangladeshi
response to our contemporary world.

THE POLITICAL DIMENSION

Bangladeshi nationalism was born in the heightened Muslim cultural and
political separatism of nineteenth and twentieth century British India and
nurtured in the Bengali struggle to retain cultural distinctiveness and share

fully the fruits of political independence and economic development in Pakistan between 1947 and 1971. Patterns of differential development between the Hindu and the Muslim communities of India during British rule, in which the Muslims lost political and economic ground vis-a-vis their Hindu neighbors, produced a defensive, then finally assertive Muslim nationalism, in Bengal no less than elsewhere. The Islamic element of Bengali Muslim identity was brought into bold relief during this period. Bengali Muslims contributed mightily to the movement for Pakistan, the political homeland for Muslims carved out of the British Indian empire in 1947, and the Muslim-majority districts of Bengal became the eastern province of Pakistan at that time. Perceived disparities in development also plagued the new Muslim state, and the Bengalis of East Pakistan came to feel that they were being given short shrift in the political and economic policies of the West Pakistan-dominated government. Differences of language and culture between the Bengalis and the ethnic groups of West Pakistan became accentuated in the context of the growing regional inequities characteristic of Pakistan's political economy. In the end the center of common allegiance to Islam could not hold against the fissiparous tendencies promoted by political and economic inequality. The reactive primordial sentiments of East Pakistanis tended to crystallize around cultural symbols, such as language, which emphasized the Bengali element in their identities. Thus *Bangladeshi* nationalism grew out of a heightened composite cultural identity, which stresses both their religious distinctiveness as Muslims in the homeland they share with non-Muslim Bengalis and the uniqueness of language and other aspects of cultural heritage which distinguish Bengali Muslims within the Islamic world.

Certainly one of the dilemmas which Bangladesh has had to face since its independence in 1971 has been to determine the degree to which Islam would be given formal expression in the legal foundation of the new state and allowed as a basis for political organization among its citizens. The Awami League government of Sheikh Mujibur Rahman, which had led Bangladeshis to independence, was from the outset determined to exclude religious considerations in the country's constitution and to prohibit political activity by its several religious groups. Thus, the 1972 Constitution of the People's Republic of Bangladesh proclaimed secularism as one of the founding principles of state policy, disallowing state favor of any particular religion, and explicitly proscribing political action by religious organizations. Islamic political parties which had been prominent in the former East Pakistan were banned.

The reasons for this early emphasis on secularism were not hard to fathom. First, the *raison d'être* of the new state was Bengladeshi nationalism, and the liberation struggle had highlighted the Bengali element in its people's cultural identity, while deemphasizing its Muslim quotient. Second, Bangladesh retained a large number of non-Muslims among its citizenry, and it was thus reasonable that the historically well-grounded potential for interreligious strife (or, in South Asian terms, communalism) be minimized by following a state policy of neutrality in religious matters. Finally, the Islamic parties had opposed the movement for autonomy and, in its final phase, independence, and many of their members were alleged to have sided with the Pakistan army during the liberation war. That they should therefore be banned, and that Islam be neutralized as a basis for law and politics, was understandable in the first years of Bangladesh's national life.

It is difficult at this juncture to assess the role of "Muslim fundamentalist" reaction to these policies in bringing about the military coup d'état which overthrew the Mujib government in August 1975. A leader of that coup has recently claimed that a desire to reconstitute Bangladesh as an Islamic state was one of its main aims, and for a brief moment during the coup an Islamic Republic of Bangladesh was actually proclaimed by the victorious dissidents over the national radio. But no official follow-up to this hasty announcement was forthcoming, and Bangladesh has remained a People's, not an Islamic, Republic.

Nonetheless, accommodation to Muslim concerns, within the framework of a gradual return to parliamentary democracy, has been apparent in Bangladesh since 1975. In November of that year another struggle within the armed forces brought to power the country's present head of state, Ziaur Rahman. In 1977, following the gradual process of consolidating his power, President Zia announced that the constitutional references to secularism as state policy would be dropped in favor of "absolute trust and faith in the Almighty Allah," and a new clause would be added stipulating that Bangladesh would "endeavor to consolidate, preserve, and strengthen fraternal relations among Muslim countries, based upon Islamic solidarity." Islamic parties, along with others reflecting the gamut of political ideologies, were allowed to function as the country groomed itself for a return to electoral rule. Large numbers of political prisoners were released at that time, activists of all persuasions, including many conservative Muslims who had been jailed by the Mujib regime for alleged "collaborationist" activities during the independence war.

The perceptible Islamic coloration Bangladesh has taken on since 1975 has not impeded the thrust for parliamentary democracy which Bangladeshis—who turn out in elections to vote in large numbers—have demanded since the days of British rule. Nor has there been a dominance of the policy by conservative Muslim forces. In the 1979 elections, which President Zia's secular and heterogeneously constituted Bangladesh Nationalist Party won overwhelmingly, an electoral alliance of Islamic parties received only 10 percent of the popular vote and gained only 20 of the 300 contested seats in the new Parliament. Thus, a majority of Bangladeshis seems unprepared at present to support an overt "Islamicization" of government which these parties stand for in varying degrees.

Meanwhile, on the international front, Bangladesh has attempted to accentuate its solidarity with the Islamic world, and the country has benefited greatly from its diplomatic association with the common concerns and multinational institutions of Muslim nations. At the same time, Bangladesh has continued to reach out to a panoply of non-Muslim Third World states and to maintain friendly ties with the major world powers. Thus, there has been an effort to mold a modern democracy while allowing full political expression to Islamic ideology, and an attempt to combine pan-Islamic solidarity with prudent flexibility in its foreign policy stance. This complex picture must surely be understood, at least in part, with reference to the history of Bangladeshi nationalism and the composite cultural character of Bangladesh as a Muslim-majority and Bengali national state.

THE DEVELOPMENT DIMENSION

A distinctively Islamic ideology has never guided national economic development policy in Bangladesh. The Zia government has moved away from the "socialist" and nationalization policies which constituted the Mujib regime's approach to development and placed greater emphasis upon the private sector and the attraction of private foreign investment. The various Muslim political parties have stressed giving an Islamic emphasis to economic policy, but, as noted above, these groups have come nowhere near the exercise of political power. Finally, from time to time one hears talk of "Islamic socialism" in Bangladesh, but it is difficult to find systematic statements about what that might entail. An important set of questions, then, may be asked as to how the social institutions of a predominantly Muslim society have reacted to governmental commitment to modernization in conventionally Western terms.

Modernization may be said to have begun in Bengal with British rule. While much of what exists in Bangladesh today in the way of modern institutions and technological infrastructure derives from the colonial encounter, the social impact of Westernizing forces was, and continues to be, as uneven as it has been complex. This is no better illustrated than with respect to educational modernization.

Western education was introduced throughout British India after 1835. Its purpose was not only the training of Indians to serve the

administrative and other institutions of colonial rule, but also the creation of
an Anglicized indigenous élite which would constitute a bulwark of support
for British government. While the Hindu community was quick to seize the
opportunities which this policy afforded, the Muslims held back. As one
of their spokesmen put it, for Muslims education meant "first religious
education, secondly moral education and lastly professional education."
A system of instruction aimed at the secular professionalization of Indians
thus held little interest for them. Throughout most of the British period,
Muslims continued to demand support for their mosque-attached
maktabs, which provided rudimentary Koranic learning to young children,
and *madrasahs*, where higher level religious education, as well as clerical
training, were imparted through the study of the Arabic, Persian, and Urdu
sacred literatures.

After 1870, Muslims finally turned to Western education in
increasingly larger numbers, but they continued to lag behind the Hindus in
this respect. Indeed, the educational disparity between the two communities
was a factor in promoting Muslim unrest and the eventual demand for
Pakistan. In 1947, relatively few of the Muslims of Bengal, compared to other
communities on the subcontinent, had received exposure to modern
education; this was one of the early problems facing Pakistan's efforts to build
a modern state.

Throughout the Pakistan period and since the independence of
Bangladesh itself, efforts have been made to expand the modern educational
base of the country. By the mid-1970s, there were some 40,000 primary
schools, 8,000 secondary schools, 600 colleges, over 60 professional schools
in medicine, engineering, law, and teacher training, as well as six full-fledged
universities, including one specializing in agricultural science. All bear the
imprint of the British, and more lately, the American educational systems,
albeit somewhat "frozen" in time and harking back to the colonial period.
This Western-derived educational system coexists with the traditional Muslim
system of the local *maktabs*, where millions of Bangladeshi boys and girls
begin their days with lessons from the Koran, and town-centered *madrasahs*
for those who seek higher levels of formal religious training.

Bangladesh does not view its commitment to educational modernization as necessarily conflicting with traditional Islamic education. Indeed,
from time to time, some efforts have been made to combine basic instruction
in Bengali language and arithmetic with the religious education of the village
maktabs, although such movements have not achieved lasting success.
Throughout the society, however, education of some sort is seen as desirable
and its attainment is consonant with social prestige and community influence.

The problems of education in Bangladesh today have little to do with
any supposed contradictions between Islam and modernization; rather they lie
in the insufficiency of resources to meet the needs. For the average

Bangladeshi child, attendance at any school is brief, and, as the country's high illiteracy rate suggests, has little lasting imprint. Not only finances, but also the family labor needs of this largely peasant society tend to keep children from moving beyond the first years of schooling. Only those from the relatively privileged rural families and the salaried urban middle and upper income groups proceed through the system and on to its colleges and universities, perpetuating a pattern of unequal access to education. A commonly acknowledged need is for the upgrading of teaching quality in all schools, whether of the traditional Islamic or non-Islamic sort. Curricula, it is widely alleged, have been hidebound since British days, taught with hopelessly outdated textbooks, and do not give sufficient emphasis to science and technical subjects. The result is production of graduates unable to find jobs and unprepared to fill the technical and professional needs of a modernizing society. Some have insisted that schools in rural areas ought to incorporate modern agricultural training, for instance, but this seems never to have been pushed at any level of the educational establishment. In short, a common criticism of Western-derived educational institutions in Bangladesh is their outmoded élitism, a holdover from the colonial period, and their failure to meet the continuing needs of the modernization process. These concerns are among the most salient in Bangladesh today.

British efforts at Westernizing education in Bengal were not matched by others in the area of agricultural modernization. The people of the former East Pakistan and today's Bangladesh inherited an agrarian situation badly in disarray. The vast majority of Bangladeshis are classic monsoon wet rice cultivators, inhabiting a deltaic land capable of producing a variety of crops during three annual growing seasons, especially if mechanized irrigation assists in the process. Agriculture, with rice as the staple and jute as the major cash crop, is the backbone of the economy, and Bangladesh's industrial sector is as yet embryonically developed. Methods of cultivation are ancient, and until recently Bangladeshi farmers have not benefited from modern fertilizers, pesticides, high-yielding plant varieties and other aids to successful farming associated with the "green revolution." The productive capacity of the means of production long ago was outstripped by an ever-burgeoning population. Further complicated by the natural vicissitudes of a monsoon climate, production failures and resulting peasant indebtedness have combined to create growing landlessness and a "rural proletariat" of day laborers and sharecroppers who compete for work on lands owned by fewer and fewer families. It is ironic to note, in the light of these grave difficulties, that Western strategies for economic growth as applied to Bangladesh from British times to date have never given agriculture a central role in the development process. No wonder that many now advocate a change in focus.

A strategy for agricultural development must rely for implementation on organizational processes and thus has to confront the "institutional factors" involved in the transformation of a traditional society. One problem Bangladesh faces in this respect is that of mobilizing people whose traditions of community life have never stressed group economic activities. Muslim peasant communities in Bangladesh have had as their main raison d'être the organization of collective spiritual life and ceremonial activities. The primary unit of community is not the local village per se, but rather the "residential brotherhood" of neighboring farmers and their families, united in common religious and ritual observance. The cultural importance of these indigenous social groupings as major vehicles for the expression of a sense of community is reflected in the most widely used Bengali name for them, *samaj*, which in its largest sense means "society" itself. *Samaj* groups do not bear a tradition of common economic endeavor among their members, and they "administrate" little in the way of "public policy" save the enforcement of Muslim codes for spiritual and ethical conduct and the settlement of local disputes. The question of mobilizing the Bangladesh peasantry, then, involves in part the adaptation of rural community institutions to the organizational tasks which modernization requires.

In certain respects, the intrinsic social solidarity that Muslim "brotherhoods" promote can lend itself to the initial formation of groups for developmental purposes. Such has proven to be the case in the efforts to establish farmers' cooperatives throughout Bangladesh, a key aspect of the country's development strategy, at least until recently. Wherever peasant cooperatives have been started, more often than not they have begun with indigenous *samaj* groups as their base. Such efforts require leadership and supervision, however. If today many observers judge the once promising cooperative movement in Bangladesh to be faltering and in disarray, it is less the fault of indigenous Muslim community institutions than of far larger problems of administration and sociopolitical organization which the people of Bangladesh are still struggling to resolve. It is likely that Bangladeshi peasants will respond to and themselves take development initiatives through the Muslim "residential brotherhoods" in which they conduct important aspects of their social life. Within such institutions, it must be noted, they commonly seek justice and remedy for their grievances, and in the past *samaj* groups have also provided a basis for collective political action. Whether and how these traditional Muslim modes of social formation will be integrated into a mass effort for change are questions of considerable interest and concern.

There have been no detailed studies of the effects of modernization on the family in Bangladesh. If urbanization is associated with the spread of modernity, then such rural-urban differences in family life as seem apparent to the casual observer may be attributed in part to the latter. In the main, the position of women in family structure suggests some of the variation. The norms of *purdah* (seclusion of women), for instance, are far more relaxed in the major cities among families at all socioeconomic levels (although some Muslims may not consider this phenomenon as a necessary feature of modernization). Education, of course, is far more widespread among women in the urban middle and upper classes, and the urban occupational structure allows for a significant degree of participation by women in a variety of professions. These phenomena do not seem to be regarded by most urban Bangladeshis as inconsistent with Islam. Typically, however, in the country-side women's work is restricted to the home environment, within which they carry out child rearing and other domestic tasks as well as important activities in the processing of agricultural goods. But, in general, it is likely that the changes that have occurred in the rural Bangladeshi family, particularly in recent decades, may be attributable to widespread poverty and population pressures, which surely have had a negative effect upon the quality of family life and the maintenance of traditional family forms.

In rural Bangladesh the peasant homestead usually houses an extended family, consisting of a multi-generational grouping of senior men, their married sons, and all their wives and unmarried dependents. Homestead land is the joint property of all the residents, but cultivation land is divided into individually owned plots, with a father characteristically keeping his farm land until death, whereupon it is bequeathed to his children. Despite the precepts of Islamic inheritance laws, most immovable property is devolved to sons, because daughters, although they may inherit, commonly move postmaritally to their husbands' homes, for which reason they either do not or are not allowed to claim land to which they might be legally entitled. Every separate landowning or otherwise economically independent subunit of the extended family constitutes a separate household within the homestead, whose members work together and share the fruits of the labor. The division of labor finds men responsible for work in the fields—planting, weeding, harvesting, etc.—with women carrying out those tasks of agricultural production which can be done within the homestead—the threshing, winnowing and husking the rice crop, in addition to cooking, cleaning, and other household chores. The norms of *purdah* are widely enforced, especially in families of relatively higher economic and social status.

In most respects, marriage customs resemble those found throughout the Islamic world. Marriages are arranged and consist of a contract between the parties, with men polygamously allowed up to four wives whom they can equitably support—in practice, though, probably no more than five percent of all households are polygamous. Bangladeshis do not evince the preference for cousin marriage found among other Muslim peoples, and commonly exercise marital options with a view to expanding their kinship networks.

Muslim family law in Bangladesh is governed mainly by Hanafite principles, but an important modification of these was attempted in the 1961 Muslim Family Laws Ordinance, enacted during the Pakistan period and still in force in Bangladesh. First, the Ordinance requires the registration of all marriages. Second, it provides that a man may marry a second wife only upon approval of an arbitration council consisting of representatives of husband and wife plus a neutral arbitrator, an elected member of the local government. Third, the law requires that reconciliatory efforts must be made before a divorce can take effect. Fourth, it allows women in polygamous marriages to grieve maintenance on the part of their husbands before an arbitrator. Finally, the Ordinance forbids the disinheritance of a man by his grandfather if both are predeceased by the man's father, which practice is allowed under traditional Hanafi law. Conservative Muslims were appalled by these changes, especially those which limited the previously untrammeled rights of men in matters of polygamy and divorce. But a study of the Ordinance's impact suggests that its main features had received at least a modicum of acceptance throughout the country by the late 1960s, suggesting that this trend would continue with further education and public awareness of the new laws.

Bangladesh, therefore, exemplifies composite cultural identity in a Muslim-majority nation-state, combining adherence to Islam with continued loyalties to an older and persisting Bengali culture. The country's national evolution and continuing political development cannot be understood without reference to that central fact. Long-standing Westernization processes in Bangladesh have been uneven in their effect, and present problems of modernization do not necessarily stem from some alleged adaptive incapacity of Islam as a socioreligious system. Indeed, Islam in Bangladesh has not only provided a source of resilience for its people against the buffeting they have received in the world order, but it has also shown an ability to coexist with modernization and itself to serve as a vehicle for change.

On May 30, 1981, Bangladesh President Ziaur Rahman was assassinated during a visit to the city of Chittagong, in an attempted coup d'etat led by Major General Manzur Ahmed, Commander of the Chittagong Division of the Bangladesh Army. Manzur apparently had hoped that other units of the armed forces would rally to his cause, but they did not. Captured soon thereafter, General Manzur was killed while being transported back to Chittagong. Manzur, whose differences with Rahman were personal, appealed to Islamic sentiment in his unsuccessful effort to mobilize support.

Vice President Abdus Sattar, a former Supreme Court Justice who is in his 70s, immediately took over as Acting President, supported firmly by General H. M. Ershad, Commander-in-Chief of the Army. Soon after taking power, Acting President Sattar announced that presidential elections would be held in six months in accordance with the Bangladesh Constitution. Although public activity surrounding the campaigning has been muted to date (July 1981)—in part because of the continuation of the mourning period for the popular Ziaur Rahman—behind-the-scenes activity and speculation have begun in earnest. If Zia's poly-stranded Bangladesh Nationalist Party remains intact, its major oppostion in the forthcoming elections probably will be the Awami League. This party is composed of supporters of former President Sheikh Mujibur Rahman, himself killed in the coup d'etat in 1975 that eventually brought Ziaur Rahman to power in November of that year.

The heterogeneous Bangladesh Nationalist Party has managed to coalesce around the candidacy of Acting President Sattar. He may be the only statesman-politician capable of holding together the diverse elements within the "umbrella party" that Zia had been able to create. Of particular interest is the role that conservative Islamic elements in the party, including several of its most potent figures, will play in the electoral campaign. In the immediate aftermath of the abortive coup, the small Islamic parties appeared inclined to support Sattar's call for broad political support of his presidency. These parties have not called for major revisions of the political order Zia put together. The Islamic states of Southwest Asia, major finanical contributors to Bangladesh, also have expressed support for Sattar's efforts to follow in the path set by Zia.

8

Sudan

EDUCATION AND FAMILY

Nafissa Ahmed El Amin

𝒯HE CONFLICT WITHIN ISLAM, which is usually expressed in terms of protracted strife between modernization and tradition, is in many ways a reflection of the impact of Western civilization on the civilization of Islam, and is only one example of the general confrontation between Western and non-Western models of society throughout the Third World. This confrontation is most pronounced in the case of Islam because of the comprehensive nature of the Islamic model and of the intensity of the pressure it has undergone as a result of the domination of the West over many parts of the Islamic World, for more than a century in some areas. The outcome as a result was neither a smooth development, in which the indigenous system has been vitalized by the impact of the Western system to develop from within, nor was it a violent upheaval in which the old system was swept away in favor of the new order. That is why the crisis of Islamic civilization is more acute than the crisis of any other civilization in the Third World.

Indicative of this fact is the marked division of some Muslim societies into two compartments living side by side, the Islamic and the Western modes of society. And this goes beyond society to stamp the character of the individual with *dualism*. This is not a healthy situation, because it is contrived and artificial and derives mainly from the physical intervention of the colonial powers which dominated many parts of the Muslim World in the nineteenth century. At that time, the Muslims were beginning to feel the impact of Western culture and were in the process of developing their own renaissance, as could be gathered from the reforms in the Ottoman Empire and in Muhammad Ali's Egypt and in the works of Afghani, Muhammad Abdu and others. The process of *ijtihad*, or moderniz-ing Islam from within by making use of new ideas and developments that do not appear to contravene Islamic principles or practice, was already gaining momentum when the colonial era put an end to it and set Muslims on a different course. The interest of the colonialists was not so much on developing the traditional society by basing their reforms on what already existed, as it was on superimposing a new model of society, based on Western lines in economics, education, law, and the like. That was easily done because most of the modern institutions in government were new to the Muslims, and their material benefits were obvious. As a result, a complete set of modern institutions was established without much reference to existing indigenous institutions or models. It is sufficient to indicate here that of the laws that governed life in Muslim society, only the laws governing family status remained basically Islamic. The others were all replaced by Western laws.

This superficial Westernization of a large part of the Muslim World was destined to falter because it was dictated in most cases by colonial or semi-colonial systems, and because it was not inherent or organic. Instead it lived tenuously side by side with whatever the ordinary Muslims regarded as their own way of life. The dichotomy seemed to work as long as the external power supported and enforced these modern institutions through education, law, and the like. But colonialism ended, and the Muslims were left on their own. They faced a dilemma over how to proceed. This dilemma lies behind the restiveness and craving for an Islamic revolution or renaissance that is sweeping through the Muslim World. The era of Western domination put an end to the earlier, healthier approach by which Islamic and Western civilizations were brushing together but making use of the contact between them to enrich and benefit each other. If this process had been allowed to continue, the development of Islamic civilization would have been more dramatic and more peaceful.

Instead, this social development was disrupted and frozen at a very critical stage, and its course was forcefully diverted from one of interaction between the two cultural systems into one in which only the Western pattern was allowed to prosper. The Islamic way of life was kept within bounds in the minds of the people and in very minor sectors of social life. Once the power sustaining this state of affairs was removed, a reversion to the earlier stage of mutual confrontation between the two civilizations was natural and impera-tive. People have to do their own homework without an overseer, especially in social and cultural development. The attempt might seem futile and unnecessary because of the energy needed to revive this Islamic way of life, after so many centuries of backwardness, and because of what has been done to the Muslim social structure by these Western institutions and practices, some of which are alien to the spirit of Islam. But the need to make that effort is felt to be a necessary sequel to political independence.

With this background in mind I intend to tackle the question of modernization and tradition in the fields of education and the family, citing examples from the Sudan. Taking education first, it must be admitted that the cleavage between education as practised in the West and that taught in the Islamic World at the end of last century was very great. Islamic education at the time stressed the religious duties of the individual, and hardly touched on the social and economic functions of the state or society. That was due to the stagnation of Muslim society, and the atrophy of the sciences linked with the growth of material life, such as architecture, engineering, farming, medicine, and the like, which had flourished during the prime of Muslim civilization between the eighth and twelfth centuries. With the decline of Muslim power and vitality, education gradually shed most of these "tool sciences," as they were known in classical Arabic, and the emphasis was laid on the pure sciences of religion as the common denominator of all Muslims. The spirit of research and criticism declined, and repetition of what had been transmitted by earlier scholars became the dominant feature of education. When modern "worldly" education was introduced into many Muslim societies, no attempt was made to link it with the earlier experience of Muslim education so that the past and the present could flow in a single channel to the future.

For Islam is essentially a religion of literacy and search after knowledge, and the Koran and the traditions of the Prophet impress on the Muslims, male and female, the need to acquire knowledge. And knowledge is not only religious knowledge, as it came to be accepted during the period of decline, when Western influence became dominant at the end of last century and the beginning of this century. The antipathy between traditional Islamic education and the earlier attempts to spread Western education was heightened by the fear of many Muslims that the purpose of modern education was mainly to corrupt Muslim youth and to divert them from their religion. Although Muslims came to realize the benefits of modern education, and to conclude that it is often, as they would say, "their own merchandise sold back to them," the rift between traditional Islamic education and Western-inspired systems of education continues. The dichotomy persists despite the many attempts at amalgamating the two systems, as can be seen in the law schools of many Arab universities where attempts are made to combine the study of Islamic and Western law, for example.

The problem in the field of education, as in most other fields, is not so much a problem of incongruence of the two systems, as it is a problem of identification, i.e., discovering the cultural identity of the community on which all social activities are to be based and achieving thereby the integration of the inherited and acquired elements of social progress. The point to be stressed is that much of what has been acquired from the West in the field of education, and in many other fields, is not inimical to Islam; otherwise it would not have penetrated so deeply into Muslim communities. On the contrary, much of it is in harmony with what Islam accepts and practices. In a recent study by the commission established three years ago in the Sudan to review Sudanese laws and to suggest revisions so that laws may come into line with the dictates of the *shariah*, or Islamic law, it was discovered that more than 80 percent of these laws, which are of English and Indian origin, do not contravene Islamic principles.

This is even more true in education, which, with only minor exceptions, is essentially a continuation of what the classical scholars of Islam had taught in the fields of mathematics, engineering, chemistry, logic, geography, and the like. The only difference is that these modern subjects are taught in isolation from the cultural background of the people concerned. Because of that, much of this teaching is looked upon as foreign and its results are suspected and rejected, especially among the common people. This is a natural sequence of social development that does not proceed from the local social base.

Although Western methods of education have been adopted by almost all Muslim countries, and are being accepted as part of their cultural heritage, there remains the problem of parallelism between this type of education and the traditional Islamic type of education. Efforts have been made in the Sudan, as in other Islamic countries, to unify the educational system so that this dichotomy between religious and secular education is abolished, but the problem lingers.

If education is to transform society and revolutionize the individual, it must be part of the personal experience of everybody. That cannot be achieved without linking the educational process with the inherited cultural experience of the people concerned, a strategy rejected by eminent imperialist administrators like Cromer, Dunlop and the like, who devised the educational system in Egypt and the Sudan at the end of the last century and the beginning of this century. Much has been done since then to harmonize the different elements in the educational process, but these attempts all fell short because an educational system cannot be enforced from without; it must spring from within. This does not amount to a rejection of Western education, but is an effort to "naturalize" it and to admit it into the mainstream of the Muslim cultural heritage. The difference might not be great, since the cultural experiences of both Western and Islamic communities are drawn from many common sources. But the process is essential if the dichotomy is to be resolved, and if organic social and cultural development of Muslim communities is to be achieved.

This is what lies behind the turmoil in many Muslim countries. It is not so much a rejection of Western achievements as it is an assertion of Muslim identity. This identity is a product of a certain tradition that has molded the character of Muslims and their society for more than fourteen centuries. Many people view this process of asserting the cultural identity of Muslim society as something hostile to the West. It is a great mistake not to realize that cultural groups aspire to be themselves after achieving political independence. It is obvious that some parts of the Western experience are destined to be rejected by Muslims as they review their experience in the colonial era, but in the long run the process is conducive to better and more amicable relations between the two communities.

Perhaps because of this situation, which still prevails in many Muslim countries, educational systems are not producing the desired effects. The problems that have accompanied the development of education in many of these countries are not due to the failure of the Islamic system as such, but to the efforts to impose a different system of education on a community with its own system of education, without reference to that local system. The method and the material of education may be the same in both cases, but some of the norms and values behind education may be different, especially because much of Western thought is loaded with materialistic elements that are not in harmony with either Christianity or Islam. This is not only reflected in thought, but in the social behavior based on it. In an integrated community where private and public behavior is guided by the same norms and where the individual is a microcosm of the community, the cultural and educational process is not divorced from its practical results, and this is evidenced by the personal behavior of the individual in society.

Because of this difference in norms, the result of Western education is not always positive, despite its many material and cultural benefits. There is, for example, an obvious undermining of social cohesion as result of fostering individuality, as against the communal spirit which Islam engenders. Much of the personal behavior which modern Western societies have come to accept is frowned on, if not rejected, by Islamic norms. All this has combined to confound the course of education under Western domination. People have suspected the motives behind this education, because they suspected its results and feared its impact on the very bases of their society. Otherwise they encouraged male and female education and sponsored its institutions from their own pockets, as can be seen in the experience of the Sudan during the Funj Kingdom between the sixteenth and nineteenth centuries, a tradition that is basically Islamic and that has persisted up to the present day in many parts of the Sudan, where there are *Khalwas*, or Koranic schools, for boys and girls separately.

The field of family life is more complicated than the field of education despite the fact that the family laws were the least affected by Western influence and were in most cases allowed to remain within the jurisdiction of *shariah* or Islamic courts. Family laws in most Muslim countries often are the only visible sign of Islam in the Muslim community. This partial application of Islam to a particular sector of social life, which is otherwise outside the jurisdiction of Islam, underlines the predicament of Islam in its own society. Misunderstanding and misconception are destined to arise from this double standard, not to mention the recurring process of judging that one system by appealing to the standards of the other, without regard to the logic of either social system.

This is quite evident in the general charge that Islam denies women their social rights, and makes them subservient to men, by tying them to the house and imposing on them all sorts of restrictions which reduce them almost to the position of chattels. Appeal is made to the seeming inequality between men and women in inheritance, where a girl receives half the amount received by her brother. All this is a result of judging the Islamic concept of society by the standards of an alien society. It is therefore proper to state the Islamic position before we can evaluate the present status of women in Muslim communities. The concept of family life in Islam rests on the assumption that men and women are the progeny of one soul (Koran 4/1, 6/98, 7/189, 39/6) and that men and women are equal human beings who are subject to the same moral and social obligations and are judged equally and by similar standards on the Day of Judgment. They are equal in humanity and complementary in function. In pursuing their social functions, the function of women is superior to that of men. That function is not restricted to the rearing of children or looking after the house, but goes beyond that to encompass all social life in the house and outside. Man, who is commanded to exert his physical energy and earn a living, is not made a master by so doing; he is a servant to woman who is performing the real work of building the social structure, which is a full time activity for which man has to pay by spending his earnings on the family.

Islam thus deems that the social function of women is the more important and can only be repaid by the work of men. The price of women's work should be provided by men. This does not mean that woman is barred from other than social work. She can do anything she likes, including earning money, but the money she earns does not belong to the family, as the man's money does; it belongs to her alone, and her husband and her family have no right to it, unless she decides to spend it on them. This is because society must pay the woman for the great work she performs as a partner in the social process; man is made to pay for that as part of the contract between the two partners. Therefore, a woman in Islam has her own individuality within the family. She does not bear the name of her husband or his family and can run her own financial matters without reference to him. However rich she may be, she can keep her wealth to herself and do with it whatever she likes. On the other hand, however poor her husband may be, he is obliged to provide her with all the necessities of life she was used to in her family's house. If she was used to servants, she is entitled to have them in her new house at his expense. A failure on the husband's part in this connection can be held against him by the wife, and she can get a divorce if she wishes.

Now because of this partnership in which the woman performs for society the actual function of society and man provides the living, it is only fair that a girl, who is legally repaid by a man for her social activity, should receive only half of what her brother receives in inheritance, simply because the money she receives is hers and does not belong to the family. The share of her brother, on the other hand, belongs to the family, and she herself is entitled to part of it because it is the duty of the brother to look after the family after the death of the father.

This system can only be judged by reference to its own functioning. Woman is not denied work as such but the type of work assigned to her, which no man can do, is deemed the real work of society; it is valued as such and can only be met by all that man can do. This is quite different from the Western concept which does not usually look at the social function of women as something that should be compensated by the labors of men. This Islamic premise secures for women legal guarantees against the whims of men, despite the fact that there is a divergence between the theory and its application. This is reflected in the respect and care that society expects a wife to receive from her husband even in polygamous marriages.

But the general breakdown of Muslim societies in modern times is reflected in the position of women as it is in the position of men. The reason for the gap between theory and practice does not lie in the observance of Islamic traditions but in the superimposition of different norms of behavior on the original Islamic patterns. It is a classic case in which two distinct cultural systems confront each other for a long period without discovering a peaceful means of mutual understanding, and neither is enriched by the positive aspects of the other.

The reason, alluded to earlier, lies in the original plan of Western colonizers to suppress the development of the traditional Islamic infrastructure and to institute their own ways of running Muslim societies. This strategy was short-lived because it could not replace the traditional Islamic system, which is so entrenched that it defies any attempt at obliteration. Once the lid of Western domination was removed, the old system reasserted itself in what we witness nowadays throughout the Muslim World. The tendency, as noted earlier, is to regard social and cultural emancipation as a prerequisite to political emancipation. Political independence necessitates the reassertion of the national tradition in all walks of life. Once this is achieved, the conflict between modernization and tradition takes a completely different course. In fact it becomes no longer a conflict, but a peaceful process of mutual give and take. Modernization in the prevailing context is taken to mean Westernization, and it is resisted as an encroachment by the West on what Musims regard as a basically distinct Muslim society, with its own philosophy and logic which are not always identical to Western norms.

Once the Muslim society is allowed to be itself by reactivating its social and culural heritage, it will devise its own ways of dealing with Western culture and civilization in a healthy atmosphere of take and give. The animosity prevailing at the moment which is intensified by political strife overshadows vast areas of cultural achievement common to both civilizations, but the Western achievements are resisted by Muslims because they would like to have these things on their own terms. A new atmosphere is needed in the work of political independence so that these nations can regain their national character which has been molested by Western domination for over a century.

The relationship betwen modernization and tradition must be transformed from the present confrontation of two apparently incomprehensible systems into a smooth process of adaptation and assimilation in which each can benefit from the useful features of the other. This is an objective for which all of us must strive if we are to enter the future as followers of the three sisterly divine religions of Judaism, Christianity, and Islam which essentially belong to the same tradition and hence have much in common. This mutual cooperation between Western and Muslim civilizations is not only vital for internal development in both areas, but it is a necessity for a unified front against the threat of atheistic doctrines to both civilizations.

9

£ibya

THE FAMILY IN MODERN ISLAMIC SOCIETY

Elizabeth W. Fernea

*T*HE ISSUE OF THE FAMILY IS BASIC IN THE DEVELOPMENT of a new Islamic society. Professor Jacques Berque (in his Foreward to André Demeersman's work, *La famille Tunisienne et les temps nouveaux*) states the problem as a struggle between old and new forms. The dispute about forms, suggests Professor Berque, is based on two rather different visions of the world.

> The traditional forms were based on ancient links with the faith. Were the new organizations, which were the result of the general historical movement, going to maintain those venerable links, or were they going to dress the same values in other clothing, or were they going to suggest new ones? In any case, their adversaries were accusing them of immorality, an unfair accusation that was destroyed by its obsession with the past. But one has to admit that Tunisia has had, and still has, difficult problems of substitution and balance.

But does the problem have to be an either/or formulation? Not necessarily. For some time, Western and Middle Eastern social scientists have tended to cast the development or decline of family structure in terms of confrontation rather than evolution. The issue of the role and status of the family, and the role and status of the members of the family, has become, from the far left to the far right, an academic battleground for staging other struggles. The familiar straw men of social science are engaged in almost holy, or at least ideological, war. Here, visible on the barricades suited (or veiled) for the fray, are: Modernization versus Tradition; Progress versus Decline; Egalitarianism versus Totalitarianism; Religious Belief versus Secularism; Marxism versus Capitalism; Men versus Women. Conflict is joined. But at the center of the struggle is the family. Far from these symbolic battles, men, women, and children in both Middle Eastern and Western society struggle on their own with economic, social, and political issues. In the lives of ordinary people, change goes on, change which is not the result of confrontation but of that creative, ancient evolutionary process known as adaptation and improvisation.

The key words here are process and confrontation. Until recently, the smoke and noise of the rhetorical battle over the issue of the decline or expansion of the family have often obscured the fact that confrontation may encourage or discourage certain kinds of actions, but that change is essentially process. Tradition, modernization, the institution of the family have been reified or deified as abstractions, rigid structures which serve as bastions for opposing forces. But tradition feeds into modernization, and vice versa. Neither exists as an entity in time and space. Process is history. It is the constant effort of human beings to establish relationships with their God, their environment, and each other, whether it be during the Industrial Revolution of eighteenth century England, the American frontier of the nineteenth century, or Mecca of the seventh century.

"Family" is a cover term which means rather different things in different societies. In the West, "family" has come to be defined simply as "parents and their children." In the Middle East, "ahl" or "ahila" is a more inclusive term and can be used to mean "relatives, family, wife, inhabitants; people, especially persons of a special group or place; members, followers; possessors." These differences must be kept in mind when the concept of family is considered. But however defined, the family is a human invention dealing with human needs, and its obvious basic functions concern the survival and reproduction of the family or family group.

Some Western social scientists are turning away from the reified and simplistic abstractions of "modernization" and "tradition." Irene Gendzier, in her general critique of modernization theory, points out the theory's "failure to explain the process of social change." But the influence of ethnocentric abstractions continues to permeate development theory, and the ideas have passed into the popular media and continue to affect Western views of the Third World. The old formulation remains close to that of Daniel Lerner, who, in *The Passing of Traditional Society*, articulated the notion that until the individual allegiance passed from the family group to the nation state (in

Turkey), that state would remain static and underdeveloped. This view—that the family in the Third World is basically a repressive force, an obstacle to change and improvement of the human condition—is expanded and enshrined in Alex Inkeles and David Smith's widely used work, *Becoming Modern.* (One of the questions addressed to the 6000 men who were interviewed in this study involved allegiance to the family group. Those who replied that their basic allegiance was to the family group were designated traditional on the scale, as opposed to modern.) Modernity was seen as a good, a prize to be won in battle. If one followed these arguments to their logical conclusion, modern man or women eventually would be alone; the network of family relationships and responsibilities, a net of restriction, would be cast off in the name of freedom. The family, according to Inkeles and Smith and Lerner, was therefore doomed, at least in its "traditional" formulation.

Of course, this has not taken place. What has happened is that Western social sciences are reexamining family theory as well as modernization theory. While Western social scientists are now divided among traditional revisionist, feminist, and Marxist views of the family, some Middle Eastern scholars have taken up arms for the "modernist" theories (as can be seen in the work of Fatima Mernissi, Hisham Sharabi, and Nawal Sadawi). At the same time, other pressures in Muslim society encourage a return to roots. The search for identity and place in a technological society involves a survey of past strengths and values, and time-tested solutions to human problems. Thus, the ideological battles over the role of the family have been moved to the Islamic world itself.

In Libya and Iran, positions on the Muslim family are hardening, enunciated in speeches and documents which are widely disseminated in the West and the Middle East. The family, as the social unit which nurtures new members and serves as a force for moral order, forms the basis not only for stated goals and ideals but for government legislation. The Iranian view may fairly be seen as restatement of older forms, somewhat like the profamily groups in the West.

The view in Libya, as set down by Colonel Muammar Qadhafi in the three Green Books, seems at first glance to be similar, though without the buttressing of *hadith,* Koranic injunction, or interpretive precedent. Read closely, however, Green Book III offers some new and imaginative approaches to détente in the battle between new and old. This is particularly vivid in the discussion of the family: "The social bond which binds together each human group, from the family through the tribe to the nation, is the basis for the movement of history . . . the social factor is a factor of survival. . . . The individual without a family has no value or social life. If human society reached the stage where man existed without a family, it would become a society of tramps, without roots, like artificial plants."

Qadhafi, along with many young Western social scientists, sees the family as a mechanism for survival and also as the foundation of a new kind of Utopian state. According to the Green Book, it is the family, together with religion, that will provide a basis for the amelioration of the human condition, as implied in the Koran. This amelioration is seen as an organic process from tradition to modernity. Qadhafi's definitions of human groups—"family," "nation," "tribe," and "society,"—are full of similes and metaphors expressing that organic, "natural" process: "Societies in which the existence and unity of the family are threatened, in any circumstances, are similar to fields whose plants are in danger of being swept away or threatened by drought or fire, or of withering away . . . . The blossoming garden or field is that whose plants grow, blossom, pollinate and root naturally. The same holds true for human society."

What does the ideal mean in practice? What of the roles of men and women? No egalitarian society is visualized here, the critics claim. States Raphael Mergui, "women have the right to liberate themselves from everything and everybody except men." The sections on women in the Green Book would certainly seem to support the traditional division of labor in the family: "Woman and man are equal as human beings . . . Why was it necessary for the existence of man and woman, rather than man only or woman only? The fact that a natural difference exists between man and woman is proved by the created existence of man and woman. This means, as a matter of fact, that there is a role for each of them, matching the difference between them." The difference is a "natural" or biological one, involving childbearing and breastfeeding on the part of the woman. "She becomes directly responsible for another person whom she helps to carry out his biological functions, without which it would die. The man, on the other hand, neither conceives nor breast-feeds. These . . . are the realities that necessitate the distinction between male and female, i.e., man and woman: they assign to each of them a different role or function in life."

The natural growth of a human being involves being socialized into the group, and this means being with the mother and the father, in the family, rather than in nurseries. For nurseries, according to Qadhafi, "are similar to poultry farms in which chicks are crammed after they are hatched. The meat of such chickens is not tasty and may not be nourishing because the chicks are not naturally bred, i.e., they are not raised in the protective shade of natural motherhood. There is no difference in human rights between man and woman, the child and the adult. But there is no absolute equality between them as regards their duties."

If we are to take these formulations at face value, how can we explain other ideological statements in the Green Books in which the revolution in Libya, the progressive ideal, is said to belong to all members of the state: men, women, and children? How can all people contribute to the new society, if half of them (women) must stay at home to fulfill their naturally designated roles as nurturers of children and maintainers of the family structure? In other words, how can one have a modern, technologically oriented society, and a people's *jamahirriya*, with full participation by all citizens if women can participate politically and socially in the functioning of the government, but without participating *publicly*? What about the work force, in which Colonel Qadhafi has suggested all Libyan citizens must participate? Are women in the home fulfilling a role in the work force? Perhaps, but events and tendencies in Libya seem to suggest otherwise.

First, women are supposed to serve in the armed forces of their country. Although the Popular Congress debated this issue at length in 1976, and no consensus was reached, women are indeed being given military training and are to be seen on the streets in uniform.

Second, women are present in great numbers in the educational system, and in the nurseries and daycare centers which exist in great profusion, at least in Tripoli. This perhaps is not surprising, except that the schools are often coeducational and men and women teachers are to be found in the same institution. Further, the principals and vice principals are often women, and the presence of many pregnant women in the school room, both teachers and students, suggests a different kind of women's role than the preliminary Green Book formulation.

Women are not seen in the shops selling goods, and only two serve in the People's Congress. Still, despite these indications of less than total participation, women are found in great numbers, in semiprivate positions in the child care centers and the schools and in public positions in the army, in the agricultural settlements, and in the bureaucracy, particularly that relating to education and agriculture. In 1978, the Minister of Agriculture was a woman. One might ask how this can be reconciled with the ideological statements about the woman's role at home as childbearer and childraiser.

If Green Book III is examined in a slightly different way, the answer may become clear. If one defines the *family* as *society*, or at least sees this as the ideal, then the family is not limited to the individual nuclear unit, found in the West, nor even to the extended family group, nor the tribal unit. The family is extended to include the wider society; it *is* the wider society: "The nation is a large family which has passed through the stage of the tribe and also through the ramifications of the tribes."

The school becomes an extension of the family (for the education of children), as then does the work place (the maintenance of the ideal society), the army (defender of the family-society), and the political arena (the working out of the ideal society). Thus, it is logical for women to participate in the wider society, for it *is* the family, and they, like men, are simply fulfilling their "natural" roles as childbearers and raisers, defenders, and maintainers of the larger family. The logical final step, although not stated in the Green Book, would be the family in its widest sense, seen as the *ummah*, the whole community of believers, the world of Islam.

From Libya, one may turn briefly to other nations such as Morocco, Tunisia, Algeria, and Egypt. Here the family structure is facing political, social, economic, and religious challenges which are less dramatically enunciated than those in Libya and Iran, but real and often bewildering. The government and religious leaders continue to espouse strong families as foundation stones of society and continue to assume that the family group is still the place where most individual problems (and many community ones) will be worked out. Given these assumptions, however, efforts are in progress at many levels to adapt tradition to changing circumstances. Confrontation tactics in this day-to-day battle have been replaced by quiet compromise and struggle. These efforts, such as the new family law recently passed by the Egyptian Parliament and the efforts to deal with the issue of polygamy in many countries, are designed, like the Green Book, to strengthen the family unit and help it continue to flourish in a changed environment. They can be seen as signposts in the fog of process, markers indicating that problems have been noted in the old formulations, that new conditions demand new solutions, and that responses are being attempted. Mediation is the keynote, rather than conflict.

Within the Muslim world today, the Islamic revival has been seen as an attempt to heal divisions caused by Westernization and colonization, and to narrow gaps between generations and classes. It is seen as a measure to establish identity. Thus, it is hardly surprising that the family becomes part of this revival, for if Islam is the soul of the Muslim world, then certainly the family group is its body. The varying formulations of family role and structure are evidence of struggle and conflict in the Muslim world, but also of immense vitality.

In the West, too, reevaluation of old social forms is under way. As this continues, our historic cultural myopia toward the social forms of other cultures (such as are found in the Muslim world) hopefully will recede. Thoughtful visionaries in both worlds are recognizing that change is process and are restating interconnections between family and society.

The British historian Lawrence Stone found the English family of past centuries to be a "searching, acting, moving institution." The Muslim family should be viewed in the same way, for obviously it is a structure flexible enough to deal with new structures and strong enough to survive change.

Part 2

Muslim Communities in Non-Muslim Countries

*T*HERE ARE MUSLIMS AND MUSLIM COMMUNITIES IN MOST COUNTRIES, but only a few nations today have large Muslim minorities. These groups are subject both to the tensions affecting the Muslim world as a whole and to the special social, economic, and political tensions inherent in being a "minority." Foremost among them are in the USSR, China, and India, and the three essays in this section discuss the situation of the Muslims in those countries.

USSR-CHINA

The Islamic concept that ideas and the pattern of daily life are strongly influenced and often dominated by religion clashes head on with the atheism of communist doctrine. This conflict gives serious problems to the Chinese and Soviet governments. Muslims are important to both countries, strategically because they form a substantial part of the population along many hundreds of miles of the sparsely populated Soviet-Chinese border area, and politically because the treatment they receive can be an asset or a liability in dealings with the Muslim world. For the Russians, there is also the important fact that Muslims constitute some 15 to 20 percent of the population of the Soviet Union, and have a relatively high rate of population growth.

Most of the Muslims in China are descendents of Arabs and other Middle Easterners who reached China hundreds of years ago and who, through intermarriage, are now largely absorbed into the Chinese population in race, language, and general culture. The Muslims who live nearer the Soviet borders, however, and virtually all of the Muslims in the USSR, are Central Asian peoples who have had little in common with either the Chinese or the Russians. Ethnically different from both, they are the descendants of nomads who swept west and south at intervals in history, and they reflect this background in culture and language—the latter being Turkic more often than not.

Both the USSR and China have given these groups variants of "national minority" status, and both governments in the 1970s seemed to be avoiding direct confrontation with them over religion. The Soviets have established an official Islamic hierarchy which deals with the Muslim world, but this structure seems to have little effect on Soviet Muslims. In both the USSR and China the numbers of functioning mosques and training schools for Islamic clergy have been drastically reduced by quiet but constant pressure.

The effect of this attrition over past years seems to have been a slippage of religious practice toward fundamentalism, but, at least in the Soviet Union, there has been no discernible decline in the volume or fervor of Islamic feeling. What this means for the future is hard to say, but current and past example leads to the conclusion that profound religious feeling stripped of intellectual content and trained religious leadership can be dangerously hard to deal with.

INDIA

Islam reached the Indian subcontinent shortly after A.D.700 when the Arabs conquered the Sind. During the next thousand years Muslim princes and dynasties gradually extended their control over most of India. When the British entered the picture in force in the seventeenth and eighteenth centuries they tended to exercise power through the principalities and political structures which were then in place. This approach helped to consolidate the position of the Muslims as rulers, in many parts of the country out of all proportion to their numbers. They often ruled over large Hindu populations, usually with Muslim-weighted military and civil staff.

The Republic of India disestablished the tradition of princely rule and established itself as a secular state, willing to recognize all religions but officially sponsoring none. For the Muslims, the practical effect of Indian policy was that their pride as members of the ruling group was shattered. Thereafter they could see themselves only as Indian citizens like the rest. This loss of position was combined with a loss of leadership; a large percentage of the Muslim intelligentsia and of Muslim officialdom moved to Pakistan during and after the bloody communal strife which accompanied partition in 1947.

The result, as Walter Andersen points out in his essay, is a Muslim minority of some 70,000,000, about 11 percent of India's population, which is disconcerted by its loss of past preference and torn between a desire, on the one hand, to be a working part of the Indian social/political world and, on the other, to be a recognized and separate religious group with special position and protection. If India can maintain evenhanded secular government in the years ahead, and can check the unacceptable incidence of communal violence which has plagued the Republic, the issue may solve itself in time. For the present, much of India's Muslim minority feels itself discriminated against or actually persecuted.

PHILIPPINES

One of the smaller minorities—the "Moros" of western Mindanao and the Sulu Archipelago in the southern Philippines—must be noted because it is the only Muslim minority currently in arms against a Christian government. The so-called Moros are Malay by race and language, like most other Filipinos, Malaysians, and Indonesians. Also, like the latter two peoples, they were converted to Islam before the Spanish occupation and Christianization of the rest of the Philippines. For centuries their ties were more toward Borneo and the Muslim areas west and southwest of their homeland than they were to Manila. In the past decade, however, the Muslim Filipinos have tended to become increasingly isolated from, and resentful of outsiders in general.

Organized on an extended family-tribe-clan basis with loose and variable intertribal relations, the Moros for centuries have resisted outside efforts to impose change that affects their daily lives, their sense of identity, and their rather simple patterns of the observance of Islam. Emphasis is put on such manly occupations as hunting, fishing, a limited number of crafts, and trade (officially called "smuggling" by national governments since the imposition of modern international boundaries). The seafarers have shared with their neighbors a temptation to piracy. Agriculture customarily has been primarily woman's work, carried out on lands to which the clan rather than the individual has traditional rights of use.

Throughout 300 years of Spanish rule, nearly 50 years of American and the first 25 to 30 years of Philippine independence, Christian-Moro relations were usually stiffly formal but acceptable, as one majority after another learned to let the Moros run their own affairs. In recent years, however, population pressure in the Philippines has produced government-supported migration from Luzon, and particularly from the over-crowded Visayas onto traditionally Moro land. Much of what the various groups of Muslims in Mindanao have regarded as their patrimony has been taken over by outsiders who have been able to obtain title deeds to it from the government.

This settlement program is regarded by the Muslims as the theft of ancestral rights and as a deliberate effort to make them a minority, both in numbers and politically, in areas they previously dominated. This process has already taken place in many parts of Mindanao. It has provoked both resentment and active resistance. This was fanned into open revolt in the early 1970s when the Marcos government undertook to apply its nationwide ban on firearms in the Muslim areas, for the Moro views his weapons as both a symbol and the guarantee of his freedom.

Christianity and Islam have combined with other factors to produce two very different cultures in the Philippines. The present conflict is the result of the clashes between these cultures rather than a direct product of conflicting religious belief. It is not unsolvable if both sides are willing to recognize each other's rights. Time is a factor, however, as the political and physical support the Muslim Filipinos receive from the Islamic world may increase pressures among the Moros to seek a solution through attempts to achieve independence rather than through regulation of the issues within a Philippine context.

UNITED STATES

There are also at least several hundred thousand Muslims in the United States. They fall into two general categories: (1) Many thousands of persons of foreign, generally Middle Eastern origin, who brought Islam with them to this country. They include a substantial number of the United States' nearly 300,000 foreign students; (2) several hundred thousand native Americans, almost all black, who have been born into or converted to Islam since the 1920s. The great majority of these Muslims live in the major cities, are adherents of one of several groups, and generally live in rather tightly organized communities. The growing importance of Islam in the United States warrants thorough and separate study since theirs are the problems of superimposing the tenents of Islam on existing culture rather than the reverse.

10

Islam

"EVEN UNTO CHINA"

Barbara L. K. Pillsbury

ISLAM IS NOT NEW TO CHINA. There have been millions of Muslims in China for hundreds of years, and today there are almost certainly more Muslims in China than in any Arab country except Egypt. Muslims live in all of China's provinces and have erected mosques in all its major cities. They are China's second largest religious group, after Buddhists, and have long outnumbered Christians. The true number of Muslims in China has been difficult to ascertain, however, and authoritative estimates have varied from 10 to 50 million.

THE HISTORICAL BACKGROUND

The story of Islam in China is an account of the movement of goods, people, and ideas during a 1300-year history of trade and conquest that spanned the breadth of Asia and extended to Africa. Chinese Muslims enjoy telling that Islam entered China by two routes. The first was by sea from the Arabian Peninsula and Persian coast through the Indian Ocean to southeast China. The second was the land route—the fabled "Silk Road"—a trade corridor that

The author wishes to acknowledge with appreciation the helpful pre-publication review of this essay by Professors Donald Leslie and Morris Rossabi and Dr. Claude L. Pickens, Jr.

extended some 6,000 miles from the eastern Mediterranean across Central Asia through Bokhara and Samarkand and eventually to Peking. There is some evidence that, by the year 622, there already existed in Canton and perhaps other nearby port cities, sizeable communities of Southwest Asians who had arrived by sea. Arab and Persian merchant ships had been plying the seas between southwest Asia and China perhaps as early as the fourth century A.D., and traders from the Arabian Hadhramaut and Persian Gulf area are thought to have settled in southeast China even before the rise of Islam. The Prophet Muhammad himself knew of China, as is indicated by one of the sayings attributed to him: "Seek knowledge, even unto China."

Twice in the eighth century (751 and 755) Arab and Persian troops were called upon to assist in Chinese battles. Many of these soldiers, rewarded with land and permission to settle it, married native Chinese women and remained in China. Chinese Muslim sources claim that Canton, by the ninth century, had a population of 120,000 Arabs and Persians.

These strangers from the West were regarded by the native Han Chinese as inferior and referred to as barbarians. Special self-administering "barbarian settlements" were established in Canton and other port cities where the "barbarian guests" were permitted to reside and to which they were obliged to confine all trading activities. Han Chinese attitudes toward the Arabs and Persians in the flourishing settlements were ambivalent. They desired their commerce and exotic goods, but resented their prestige and prosperity. Twice during this period (in 760 and 878), several thousand Arabs and Persians fell victim to anti-foreign sentiment and were massacred by Hans. This period (the duration of China's Tang dynasty, 618-905) is referred to by many present-day Muslim Chinese as their "period of penetration."

This was followed by the "period of expansion" corresponding to China's Song, Yuan, and Ming dynasties (960-1644). Arab and Persian merchants continued coming in great numbers to southern coastal ports during the Song dynasty, and Muslim merchants of various ethnic and tribal backgrounds served as intermediaries in the overland Silk Road trade. Muslims gained yet a firmer foothold when China was conquered by the Mongols of Central Asia whose leader Khubilai ("Kubla Khan") founded the Yuan dynasty.

The Mongols developed a program of "nationality legislation" that divided the population of China into three groups: the Mongols were on top, Muslims and Central and West Asian immigrants formed a privileged second class, and Hans were on the bottom. Persian, the lingua franca of Central Asia and of the Westerners of China, was a major language of the Mongol administration. Muslims directed the financial administration of the empire and were appointed to high positions in the central government. According to Chinese Muslim sources, nine provincial governors were Muslims. Throughout this period the Muslim population expanded territorially and in numbers, and growth ocurred not only through immigration but also through intermarriage with Han women and the frequent adoption of Han children.

During the Muslims' first seven centuries in China they remained a distinctly foreign minority with foreign connections. Beginning in the fourteenth century, however, they became increasingly isolated from the rest of the Muslim world as Han potentates replaced the Mongols as China's emperors and, in reaction to the Mongols, sought to wipe out foreign influence. The Han emperors prohibited the use of foreign languages, names, and clothing inside China and banned foreign travel. In addition, discovery of the sea route to India by Vasco de Gama wrought a heavy blow to the Muslim sea trade, and eventually it was brought to a complete end as the Europeans gained control of the Far East trade.

From the fourteenth through the nineteenth centuries, then, Muslims in China had relatively little direct contact with the rest of the Muslim world. It was rare that any of them made the pilgrimage to Mecca or that foreign Muslims visited China. Instead the Muslims of Arab-Persian descent became acculturated through adoption of Chinese surnames, clothing, and food habits, and the continued marriages to and adoption of the native Hans. Gradually Chinese dialects replaced Arabic and Persian not only as a means of communication with the Hans, but among the Muslims as well. As a result of this sinification the Muslims were no longer referred to as "Arabs," "barbarians," or "foreigners," but came to be known as *Hui-hui*, or *Hui*, (pronounced "Hway") the name by which they are known today.

A third period of Muslim history in China is referred to as the "period of weakness," or "period of calamity." It corresponds to the Qing dynasty (1644-1911) when China was once again conquered by nomadic foreigners from the North, this time the Tungusic-speaking Manchus. Unlike the Mongols, the Manchus had no experience with or understanding of Muslims; when they needed assistance in administering the empire they turned to the Hans.

The Manchus adopted segregationist policies (including forbidding Muslims to own land or live within the walls of a city), and they began annexing and exerting control over eastern Turkestan where the Central Asian Muslims were dominant. Additionally stimulated by widespread economic duress, ethnic conflict between Hans and various Muslim minorities became commonplace. Officials submitted appeals to the emperors demanding that the Muslims be "de-Muslimized," or at least "strictly punished and placed under restraint." A bloody series of Muslim uprisings and rebellions that persisted, despite official and military suppression, from the seventeenth through the early twentieth century brought death to millions of Hans and Muslims alike.

The fourth, or "renaissance," period of Chinese Muslim history began in 1912 when the Manchu emperors were defeated, the imperial system destroyed, and a new Western-type republican government established. This government formally identified Muslims as one of China's "five great peoples" (usually translated, erroneously, as "races"), and created a new flag with five stripes of equal width, a white stripe symbolizing the Muslims. Much confusion ensued over whether this stripe symbolized all Muslims in China and, if so, whether the Muslims were "all one race," or were "many races," or "just Chinese with a separate religion."

Like Hans during this pre-1949 republican period, many Muslim Chinese became actively engaged in such reforms as the introduction of Western educational curricula. Larger numbers of Muslims again began making the pilgrimage to Mecca and several dozen studied at al-Azhar University in Cairo. During the 1930s and 1940s, China's Nationalist Party, the Chinese Communist Party, and the Japanese all sought to win the loyalty of the Muslims and thereby the control of the long portion of the strategic Sino-Soviet border area dominated by the Muslims.

MUSLIMS IN CHINA TODAY

In the People's Republic of China Muslims are dealt with not only in terms of religious policies but also according to a set of "minority nationality" policies. Following the Soviet example, China's Communist leadership has identified over fifty ethnic groups as minority nationalists (which, it says, occupy about 60 percent of China's total land area). Of these, eleven are Muslim—"by blood" even if not by current practice of Islam. Virtually all are sunnis of the Hanafi school of jurisprudence, though this distinction has little significance in China. Nine of these Muslim minorities are of Central Asian derivation, speak Central Asian languages, and live in Xinjiang province (which is geographically part of Central Asia) or in adjacent provinces of northwest China. Six of the nine speak Turkic languages, and of these all but one have fellow ethnic group members in the Soviet Union. Two speak Mongolian languages, the Tajiks speak an Iranian language, and the recently identified Tujia of central China speak a Tibeto-Burman language.

The largest of the eleven groups, however, are the Huis, the Chinese-speaking Muslims who claim descent from the Arab and Persian merchants, mariners, and militiamen who settled in China centuries ago. Of the eleven Muslim minorities, the Huis are the most acculturated to Han ways, are the only one that is distributed throughout all provinces of China, and the only one that speaks Chinese as a mother tongue. Most Huis appear physically similar if not identical to the Hans, and are culturally similar in many ways. Indeed, most Huis are more similar to Hans than they are to China's other Muslim minorities and certainly than they are to present-day Arabs or Iranians. Huis agree they are Chinese citizens, but insist they are not Hans. Huis explain that they are not simply Chinese who happened to convert to Islam, since they have foreign blood (and specifically "Arab blood") which Hans do not. Hui identity is thus not just a matter of religious belief but of "blood." In this sense, even Huis who never pray or go to a mosque, or who describe themselves as "not religious," can still be regarded as Huis.

Huis generally do not eat pork (and often avoid other "Han food" as well in the belief it has been contaminated by pork), they are generally endogamous, and they have traditionally lived apart and otherwise maintained social distance from the Hans. Huis also differ from Hans in that they have traditionally refused to participate in "Han religion" (the amalgam of Confucian-laced Buddhism, Taoism, folk religion, and "ancestor worship" that has been fundamental to Han culture and social organization) but that Huis regard as idol worship and therefore forbidden by Islam. Thus, traditionally, Huis were stigmatized as deviant, if not amoral, for failing to adhere to the Han cultural norms (such as rituals honoring ancestors) and characterized as peculiar for aspects of their own culture (such as use of a "secret" language—Arabic—and avoidance of pork). Today Huis are no longer blatantly discriminated against, but some stigmatization and stereotyping continue.

The number of Muslims in China today remains uncertain, just as the Chinese population as a whole defies precise estimation. Both the number of Muslims and the nature of Muslim identity have been subjected to considerable political manipulation and remain a matter of disagreement. It was the government of the Republic of China that promulgated the doctrine and national flag identifying Muslims as one of China's "five great peoples." Later it proclaimed that Chinese Muslims were not a separate people, but only followers of a separate religion, and in 1936 it published provincial statistics showing a total of 48,104,240 Muslims. This figure has been widely cited ever since with the result that "about 50 million Muslims in China" became a commonly accepted estimate.

Following the 1949 Communist takeover, the government of the People's Republic of China put forth a new definition—that the Muslims were not one but many separate peoples and that they totaled only 10 million. This, plus accounts of killings and persecution of Muslims during the early years of the regime, led many outside observers to ask what had happened to the "missing 40 million," and to conclude that the answer was either genocide, forced conversion, failure to admit a Muslim identity to officials for fear of discrimination or persecution, or, alternatively, that the original figure of 48 million had been too high. The Peking government continued to put forth the same figure of "about 10 million Muslims" from the early 1950s through the late 1970s despite the near doubling in the interim of China's total population and the reportedly higher levels of fertility among the minority peoples. At present Peking gives 13.9 million as the total number of Muslims in China. Cautious speculation, however, suggests that a figure of 20 to 30 million Muslims might be closer to the truth.

The most obvious manifestations of Muslim presence throughout China are the ubiquitous Hui (non-pork) restaurants and, in major cities, special "Hui products" stores. Questioning reveals that most factories maintain special cafeterias for their Muslim workers and the official press occasionally publishes such items as "10,000 Huis working in factories, enterprises, government offices, schools, and other institutions [in such-and-such a city]."

Little information has been published about the actual conditions of Muslims in the People's Republic today, but they appear to have received better treatment during the past three decades than other religious groups. In part this is because of their strength along the Sino-Soviet border, and because the government has regarded them as important in its relations with Arab and other Islamic nations. It also is because the Muslims have been dealt with primarily as national minorities, rather than as a religious group, and thus have been accorded certain privileges, such as being permitted to proceed more slowly than Hans in land reform and family planning.

Of five autonomous regions the government established to curry favor with the minorities, two bear the names of Muslim minorities; they are the Xinjiang Uygur Autonomous Region and the Ningxia Hui Autonomous Region. Counties and districts with large Muslim populations have also been given nominal autonomy and named after the respective minority. Not all Muslims live within those nominally Muslim areas, however, and not all people there are Muslims. Moreover, since the establishment of the "autonomous" areas the proportion of Muslims in them has actually decreased as a result of the government's transferring and resettling large numbers of Hans in minority areas to increase official influence over the minorities and to hasten their acculturation. Thus, while Muslims in these areas receive special consideration (e.g., inclusion in local party and government structures), autonomy remains largely nominal.

The 1954 Constitution proclaimed a policy of religious freedom—by which is meant "freedom to believe and freedom not to believe." For Chinese in general this usually means that older people may continue to believe but that young people generally find it in their best interest not to believe. The number of functioning mosques in China is not stated anywhere, although government sources frequently mention sixty-seven mosques in Peking.

Many mosques were closed in the early 1950s, however, and remain closed; they are used for non-religious purposes or for such quasi-religious purposes as a Muslim bakery or Muslim "funerary procedures office." Some of the famous old mosques of the major cities have remained open for much of the last three decades (with the general exception of the 1960s Cultural Revolution period), have been renovated with government funds, and today, given the modernizing policies of Deng Xiaoping, are frequented by larger numbers of Muslims than in the past when Mao's rigid policies prevailed.

Much Islamic activity that was formerly a private matter (such as saving funds for and making the pilgrimage to Mecca), or was organized by local religious leaders (e.g., nearly 100 different Muslim periodicals before 1949) has become official activity. The traditional mosque schools, as well as the Islamic primary, secondary, and teacher training schools that Muslims had established in the first part of this century, had apparently been closed by the 1960s, and special official schools and institutes set up instead. These include the Institute of Muslims established in 1949, the Central Institute for Nationalities founded in 1951 with eight branches in minority areas, and the Islamic Theological Institute in 1955. A Chinese Islamic Association was also founded in the early 1950s under government support. The Association has produced a new Chinese Koran, entertains and maintains relations with foreign Muslims, has published or probably passed judgment on the meager literature that has appeared about Muslims and Islam since 1949, and helps organize annual government-sponsored *hajj* delegations to Mecca.

These official bodies have permitted the Chinese government to claim favorable treatment of the Muslims, while taking forceful measures to redistribute mosque lands (*waqf*) and to wrest control of Muslim communities from the *ahongs*, the traditional religious leaders. Through at least the 1960s, Muslims occasionally protested such measures by organized dissent. In Honan province, for example, Muslims in 1953 proclaimed an "Independent Islamic Kingdom," asserting that they were Muslims first and Chinese second, that their first language was Arabic, and that their loyalty was to Mecca and not to Peking; Peking Muslims rebelled during the Cultural Revolution of the 1960s.

Islam's future in China is difficult to predict, but the past suggests important clues. The Hans have a history of assimilating non-Han people. This has to do both with Han culture and with policies pursued by various regimes. The Chinese Jews, for example, became assimilated after about a thousand years in China once they had adopted Chinese as their lingua franca and once contacts with foreign Jews had been brought to an end leading to a situation in which destroyed synagogues were not rebuilt, no new rabbis were trained, and intermarriage with Hans became commonplace.

Also by way of example, today in Taiwan, a population that is descended from Huis who migrated from the mainland three centuries ago is similarly on the verge of assimilation. This process began under Japan's 1895-1945 occupation government whose policies against the practice of "foreign religions" led to a severing of contact with Muslims outside Taiwan, the abandonment of whatever mosques existed, the cessation of the training of religious leaders, and instead much intermarriage with Taiwanese Hans.

Chinese annexation of eastern Central Asia during the eighteenth century brought new foreign Muslims—Turkic peoples—into the Han-ruled state. Their position in Chinese society resembles somewhat that of the Muslims of Arab and Persian background at the time China's Ming emperors forbade foreign influence; today Turkic Muslims in Chinese still speak their Turkic native languages, but Chinese is spreading among them and the government has introduced writing systems for the Turkic languages intended to hasten the adoption of Chinese and promote assimilation. The Turkic minorities have maintained mosques and continue to train religious leaders, although considerably constrained by Peking policy and strategy. Intermarriage with Hans is reportedly increasing due to the massive transfer of Hans into Turkic territories, and in recent decades the government has sought to curtail communication with Turkic neighbors outside China.

Will China's Muslims go the way of the Chinese Jews and early Taiwanese Muslims? Chinese policies are designed to bring this about through the process of cultural assimilation. It may be that world political developments and new technologies of the twentieth century are introducing factors that will prevent the old process of sinification from taking its toll on the eleven Muslim minorities in China today. In any case, assimilation of the Turkic minorities, which remain relatively unacculturated to Han ways, probably will not occur in the near future. Assimilation is much more likely, although by no means certain, for the already highly acculturated Huis, among whom young people have been raised under socialism and appear to have little understanding of Islam and little of the Islamic sentiment that drew so many of their parents and ancestors together against the Han Chinese.

11

Islam in the Soviet Union

Alexandre K. Bennigsen

℃HE MUSLIM COMMUNITY OF THE SOVIET UNION, 44 million strong in 1979, is divided into three main ethnic groups: Turks—37 million, Iranians—3.6 million, Ibero-Caucasians—3 million. These groups are distributed among three principal areas (1979 figures): Central Asia— 27 million, Caucasus—10 million, Middle Volga, Urals, and Western Siberia—7 million.

Central Asia is the most important Muslim area of the USSR. Its southern part (south of Syr Darya) was conquered by the Arabs in the seventh and eighth centures; by the middle of the tenth century Islam had become the only religion of the territory. Except for the members of a small Jewish community in Bukhara (some 30,000 persons in 1970), all traces of pre-Islamic civilizations (Buddhist, Manichean, and Nestorian) have disappeared. Between the tenth and the late eleventh centuries, Central Asia was one of the most prestigious cultural areas of the Muslim world.

The two great non-Muslim invasions from further east in Asia— those of the Kara Kitay, in the twelfth century and of the Chingissid Mongols in the thirteenth—did not affect the Muslim character of this region.

In the northern part of Central Asia—the Kazakh steppes and the Tian-Shan mountains (Kirghizia)—the progress of Islam was slower. It was introduced in this area from two directions and in two sucessive waves:

1. from the South, in the fourteenth and fifteenth centuries, through the missionary activity of the sufi brotherhoods (*tariqats*), especially of the *Naqshbandiya* order;

MUSLIM AREAS O

BLACK SEA

Kazan

Don River

Volga River

BASHKIRI

CAUCASUS MOUNTAINS

GEORGIA

TURKEY

ARMENIA

SYRIA

AZERBAYJAN

CASPIAN SEA

KAZA

ARAL
SEA

Syr Darya River

TURKISTAN*

Urgench

ASHHABAD*

BUKHARA

Ashhabad*

IRAN

Charjow*

Bukhara

CHARJOW*

Samarkand

AFGHANISTAN

PAM

c. finlayson

THE SOVIET UNION

*The following locations have different modern names and/or spellings:

Charjow = Chardzhow
Ashhabad = Ashkhabad
Bashkiria = corresponds roughly to Bashkir A.S.S.R.
Turkistan = corresponds roughly to Turkmen S.S.R.

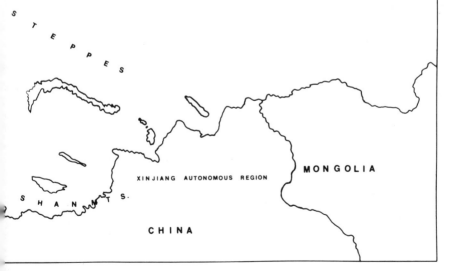

M T S.

W E S T E R N

S I B E R I A

U. S. S. R.

S T E P P E S

XINJIANG AUTONOMOUS REGION

MONGOLIA

S H A N M T S.

CHINA

2. from the northwest, in the sixteenth and seventeeth centuries,
   through Kazan Tatar merchants and *ulemas*.

Until as recently as the Second World War, however, the former
nomads, both Kazakhs and Kirghiz, were but superficially Muslim. Their
"Islamization" was thoroughly completed only in the post-war period by the
Qadiri tariqat brought into Kazakhstan by the North Caucasians whom the
Russians had deported.

Turkistan, formerly an Iranian area, was "Turkicized" over the
centuries. Surviving there is an Iranian group of three million, the Tajiks, in
the mountains of the southeast. There are also other small, non-Turkic groups:
the Central Asian Arabs, believed to number less than 20,000; the Chinese
Muslims (Dungans), 52,000 in 1979; recent immigrants from Iran: Kurds,
40,000 in 1979; Baluchis, 13,000 in 1979.

Sunni Islam of the Hanafi school predominates in Soviet Central
Asia, although there are some 40 to 60,000 Ismailis (heterodox shiites) of the
Nizarite sect in the Gorno-Badakhshan Region (the Pamirs). Shiah Islam is
also represented by some 70,000 followers who live in such cities as
Samarkand, Bukhara, Urgench, and Charjow. There was a small colony of
Bahais in Ashhabad.

Central Asia possesses a strong historical-cultural unity. After the
Arab conquest, it was usually a unified empire, and when it was divided, this
was done along political-geographic lines, never by ethnicity.

Eastern Transcaucasia (present-day Azerbayjan) was conquered by
the Arabs in the seventh century; by the eighth century most of the population
was Muslim. Living among them were small islands of non-converted Jews
("Dagh-Chufut": 40,000 remaining in 1970) and Christians (6,000 Udins in
1970) that have survived to this day.

The westward movement of the Arabs into the Caucasus, however,
was checked by two powerful Christian bastions (Georgia and Armenia).
North of Transcaucasia, the Arabs did not break through the barrier
established by the Jewish Khazars beyond Derbent. Eastern Transcaucasia
remained a mixed Iranian Iberic area until the eleventh to the twelfth
centuries, when it became thoroughly "Turkicized" with the arrival from the
East of the Turkic Seljuk tribes.

Unlike what happened in Azerbayjan, the penetration of Islam into
the mountains of the north Caucasus was slow. While the Arabs had reached
Daghestan in the seventh century, it was only late in the sixteenth that the
central Caucasus (Kabarda) adopted Islam. The Chechens became Muslims in
the eighteenth century and some Cherkess tribes only as recently as
the nineteenth.

By contrast with Turkistan, Transcaucasia presents a rich religious
variety. Since the late fifteenth century, shiism has been the dominant creed:

70 percent of the Azeris—about 4 million— are Shiahs. Sunnism of the Shafai school prevails in northern Azerbayjan, and there are isolated groups of Ali Ilahis (heterodox shiites), of Bahais, and even of Yazidis (ultra-shiites) in Soviet Armenia. The northern Caucasus, however, where Islam was introduced mainly by sufi *tariqats*, is sunni territory (Shafii in Daghestan; Hanafi elsewhere).

The Caucasus is an extraordinary mosaic of races and languages; Islam is the only unifying bond. Muslims in the Caucasus belong to three ethnic groups: (1) Turks (Azeris, Kumyks, Nogays, Balkars, Karachais)—6 million; (2) Iranians (Ossetians, Kurds, Talysh, Tatis)—800,000; (3) Ibero-Caucasians (Daghestanis, Chechens, Ingush, Kabards, Cherkess tribes, Abkhaz, Abazas, Georgian Muslims)—3 million.

Culturally and politically, Shiah Muslim Transcaucasia has been part of the Iranian world. On the other hand, the northern Caucasus (especially Daghestan and the Chechen country) has been an area of Arabic culture since the eighteenth century; until 1917, classical Arabic was used there as the only literary and inter-tribal spoken language. In our times, the northern Caucasus remains a bastion of conservative and militant Islam, represented by two very active sufi brotherhoods: the *Naqshbandiya* and the *Qadiriya*.

The Middle Volga accepted Islam in the ninth century when the King of Bulghar was converted by the Caliph's ambassador. After that, the Middle Volga was an important center of Muslim culture. Bulghar survived the Mongol invasion of the thirteenth century and in the fourteenth Islamized the Golden Horde. It is from Bulghar (replaced in the fifteenth century by Kazan) that Islam penetrated into the steppe region north of the Black Sea, into the Ural mountains (present Bashkiria) and into western Siberia. The Tatar Muslims of the Volga were conquered in the middle of the sixteenth century by the Russians who endeavored for three centuries, without success, to destroy or to assimilate them. The Tatar reaction to this pressure took the form of the "Tatar Renaissance" of the nineteenth century. At the turn of the century, the Volga Tatar modernists, the *jadids*, were the unquestioned political and cultural leaders of all Russian Islam.

With the conquest of Kazan in 1552, Russia began its imperial expansion eastward and southward, incorporating Muslim territories. This progression continued until the early twentieth century, when Russia occupied the Pamirs.

The Imperial Russian government applied to the Muslims two extreme methods: assimilation and segregation. Assimilation was applied systematically, where the Volga Tatars were concerned, between the sixteenth and the late nineteenth centuries. Conversion to Orthodox Christianity was considered the best channel for russification. Segregation, complete intellectual and political separation, was applied in the northern Caucasus and in

Central Asia after the conquest of these areas in the latter half of the nineteenth century. More liberal policies were applied in the Crimea, the Kazakh steppes, and Azerbayjan.

The two extreme methods were inefficient. Assimilation failed, producing a deep and lasting xenophobia. Apartheid was a hopeless endeavor.

Nevertheless, at least part of the Muslim population of the Russian Empire (especially the Tatars) for centuries was in close contact with the Russians. This closeness to a technologically more advanced civilization left a deep imprint on the Muslims and differentiated them from their brethren abroad.

Russian Muslims, the first Muslims to be conquered by a Christian power, were also the first to react against their conquerors. Their reaction may be summarized as follows:

- Muslims imitated the superficial aspects of Russian (and European) civilization, while trying to catch up with its intellectual and material superiority. The Tatar *jadid* reformism developed under the influence of Russian liberalism, although the religious basis of the Muslim culture was never questioned. No one—not even the Muslim Bolsheviks—dared to attack Islam until the 1917 Revolution.
- Russian culture served as a channel through which Muslims hoped to acquire Western and Central European culture, a more important model than the Russian one. *Jadid* reformism bears the brand of the French Revolution, English liberalism, and German romanticism.
- The Russian ideological imprint was limited to the influence of Russian populism, with its "going to the people" trend. Later, at the beginning of the twentieth century, the tendency appeared to imitate the Russian forms of socialism, the Socialist Revolutionary Party, and Bolshevism.
- When Muslims began to borrow Russian political theories—and, after 1905, their methods of organization—their object was less to draw closer to the Russians than to acquire the weapons with which to fight them.

ISLAM UNDER SOVIET RULE

Since the 1917 Revolution, Islam in the Soviet Union has confronted Marxism-Leninsim, a totalitarian ideology which aspires, *inter alia*, to reduce

Islam to a "private affair." The "Islamic policy" of the Soviet regime pursues a single goal: the elimination of religion from Soviet society. This policy may be summarized as encompassing the following elements:

- Radical secularization aiming at the disappearance of the Muslim religious establishment. The means to this end are propaganda and administrative measures. All *shariah* courts, *waqfs*, and religious schools disappeared in 1928, and the number of mosques has been reduced from over 24,000 in 1913 to about 300.

- Accelerated modernization through settlement of the nomads (the Kazakh population decreased from four million to slightly over three million between 1926 and 1939), the industrialization of Muslim territories, and an attempt to break up the Muslim family.

- "Social engineering" from above, including the elimination, between 1928 and 1940, of the pre-revolutionary "bourgeois" or "aristocratic" Muslim élite and its replacement by a new Communist élite of peasant origin.

- Control over the surviving religious establishment. What remains of the Islamic establishment is treated as a regular "Church"—a unique situation in the Muslim world. Soviet territory is divided between four Muslim Spiritual Boards, each chaired by a *mufti*. The most important has the title of the "Great Mufti" of Central Asia. The muftis have the right to appoint "clerics" and to control the "working mosques," and they, in turn, are controlled by the Council for Religious Affairs of the Central Committee of the Communist Party of the USSR.

This ecclesiastical hierarchy is loyal to the Soviet government. It does not protest against unrelenting anti-Islamic propaganda or the closing of mosques. It provides valuable help to the Soviet government in spreading propaganda abroad, especially as "ambassadors" to the Muslim world, and in acting as "moderator" in the USSR.

How has this policy, pursued over 60 years, affected Soviet Islam? All official Islamic religious life is kept under strict control by the Soviet government, operating through the four "Spiritual Boards" which provide an imposing facade. The Board of Tashkent is the center of numerous international Islamic conferences and hosts countless religious delegations from abroad. Nevertheless, behind the spectacular scenery set up to demonstrate to the world at large the freedom and prosperity enjoyed by Soviet Muslims, the reality is wretched. There are today no more than a few hundred mosques (fewer than 150 in Central Asia), two *medreses* in (Bukhara and Tashkent), one religious periodical (*Muslims of the Soviet East*), published in Arabic, English, French, Persian, and Uzbek in Arabic script, three or four editions of the Koran since the Second World War and one edition of al-Bukhari's collection of *hadith*. The number of "registered" clerics probably does not total more than 1,000.

"Official" Islam, on its face, should not have been able to maintain even a veneer of Islam among the population, which long ago should have fallen into ignorance and indifference. Paradoxically, however, recent Soviet surveys reveal that the "level of religiosity" remains exceptionally high among Soviet Muslims: 80 percent of the population is said to belong to various categories of "believers," whether "by personal conviction," "tradition," or "under pressure."

According to the definition of Soviet sociologists, a "believer" is a person performing certain rites and following certain customs of religious origin. But even the 20 percent of Soviet Muslims who are "official" atheists observe some religious rites, though these have lost their spiritual significance and are considered "national" rather than religious customs. These rites apply to burials in Muslim cemeteries (observed by all of the population), to circumcision (also observed by everyone), and to religious marriage (80 percent). Indeed, there are no "absolute atheists" among Soviet Muslims. Even official non-believers participate in important religious festivals (Kurban Bayram, the festival of sacrifice, for instance) because they are deemed to be "Turkmen" (or "Uzbek," etc.) occasions.

Soviet sources reveal that in the areas where the Soviet authorities have tried to destroy Islam by closing all the mosques, religious practice has reached a high level. This is the case in the Chechen-Ingush Republic in the Caucasus, where all mosques were closed in 1943 but which remains the bastion of militant religious conservatism, and in the Turkmen Republic, where, in 1978, there were only four village mosques. According to recent Soviet surveys, this paradox is explained by the phenomenon that Soviet literature calls "Parallel Islam." On one hand, there is the unorganized mass of "firm believers," who belong to the older generation, who speak and read Arabic, and who possess a rudimentary knowledge of Muslim theology. In such areas as the Caucasus and the former nomadic regions of Central Asia, the traditional institutions—the Council of Aqsaqals, the Clan Courts, and the councils of tribal leaders—have preserved their authority and prestige, and help to maintain the high level of religious belief and practice. On the other hand, four well-organized and disciplined semi-clandestine Sufi brotherhoods (*tariqats*), more influential now than 50 years ago, are especially active in the USSR: the *Naqshbandiya* (in the Caucasus and in all of Central Asia), the *Qadiriya* (in the northeastern Caucasus with new implantations in Central Asia since the Second World War), the *Khalwatiya* (in Turkmenistan), and the *Yasawiya* (in Kazakhstan, Kirghizia, and Uzbekistan). Sufi orders are particularly busy in former nomadic areas, where they have been superimposed on the clan tribal system of the society.

In spite of the efforts of the Soviet government, Islam remains the unifying bond among various "Muslim peoples." The word "Muslim" is frequently used to designate a national origin. The often-heard expression "a non-believing Muslim" is not a paradox. Soviet Islam today is much different from the progressive, liberal, modernish prerevolutionary *Jadidism*. It is a conservative creed that is undergoing a process of traditionalist revival similar to that which is found today in many other Muslim countries. This revival, however, is a local phenomenon that owes nothing to influences from abroad. Sufism, which ecompasses a search for purity, an intolerance of "bad Muslims," and a rejection of the "Infidels," plays a major part in this revival. It is a safe assumption that sufism saved Islam in the Soviet Union during the darkest years of the antireligious campaign.

Soviet Islam had been isolated from the rest of the Muslim World for more than half a century. The pilgrimage to the Holy Places of Mecca and Medina was limited to some 30 pilgrims per year, and the pilgrimage to the shiah holy cities in Iraq and Iran was forbidden. Official contacts were resumed in the late 1960s, but on a very limited scale: Muslim religious officials were sent abroad, and several tightly controlled international conferences were organized by the *mufti* of Tashkent to demonstrate his loyalty to the Soviet government and to prove that USSR is a better friend of Islam than the "imperialistic" West.

The war in Afghanistan brought a dramatic change. The Soviet force which invaded Afghanistan in December 1980 had a relatively high proportion (up to 40 perent) of Muslims from Central Asia. We do not know whether these troops were supposed to fight the rebels and to pacify the country, or whether they were brought to Kabul simply to give the Soviet invasion a "Muslim profile." In any event, the Muslim soldiers were "unreliable" and were pulled out of Afghanistan in February 1980. Since then, the Soviets who are fighting the Afghan rebels are Russians, and the war has assumed the character of a colonial war (for the Russians) and of a Holy War (for the Afghans).

Soviet Muslims are still numerous in Afghanistan, as of mid-1981, from the level of the ambassador (a Volga Tatar) to that of the truck driver. Individuals are circulating, as well as rumors, information, and ideas. The iron curtain has been lifted, and it is not possible to hide from Central Asians that a war is being waged in Afghanistan and that Russians are slaughtering Uzbeks, Tajiks and Turkmens there. One and a half million Uzbeks, 3 to 4 million Tajiks, and about 200,000 Turkmens, all closely related to Soviet Central Asians, are participating actively in the rebellion.

It is logical to assume that the Afghan war has a direct impact on relations between the Russians and Central Asian and Caucasian Muslims. The heroic resistance of the Afghan *mujahidin* (strugglers for Islam, freedom fighters) already has demonstrated that the Russians are not invincible, and the struggle eventually may spill over into Central Asia and the Caucasus.

Two ominous incidents took place in Central Asia in 1980. One is directly related to the Afghan tragedy; the other may be an indirect consequence of it.

- In March 1980, riots broke out in Alma-Ata, the capital of the Kazakh Republic, when the local Muslim population refused to let Soviet authorities bury the bodies of Kazakh soldiers killed in Afghanistan in a Russian military cemetery.
- The second incident, the assassination in December 1980 of Sultan Ibrahimov, a high-ranking member of the Communist Party and Chairman of the Council of Ministers of the Kirghiz SSR, cannot be regarded with certainty as a consequence of the Afghan war. Official Soviet sources called it "a politically motivated provocation," which means nothing. According to rumors in Moscow, Ibrahimov was murdered by "Muslim nationalists." This term may well refer to the members of a sufi brotherhood especially active in Kirghizia.

The reactions of the Soviet authorities to the possible effect of the Afghan and Iranian revolutions on Soviet Muslim territories prove that they are taking this danger seriously. References to the subversive activity of "foreign spies and agents" and of the "reactionary sufi groups" have become numerous over the last six months, as have the appeals to the K.G.B. and the Border Guards protecting Soviet southern borders to be vigilant.

The most significant manifestation of concern was an article by Major-General Z. Yusif Zade, Chairman of the Azerbayjan SSR K.G.B. in *Bakinskii Rabochi* (Baku, December 19, 1980). The General denounced the infiltration of foreign agents and "the antisocial" activity of the *sectarians* (a term usually employed in Soviet political literature to designate the members of Sufi orders) and of the "*reactionary Muslim clergy*" (another term for Sufis).

It is, of course, too early to reach conclusions about the impact of the Afghan war and of various Muslim fundamentalist movements on Soviet Islam, but is possible to discern trends:

- It seems probable that in the not-too-distant future the Soviet authorities will attempt once again to isolate their Muslim territories from the Muslim World to prevent ideological contamination.
- A new wave of religious persecutions (a "campaign against

banditism and hooliganism") directed essentially against Parallel (Sufi) Islam is already in progress.

- Soviet authorities are tightening their control over the official Islamic establishment. During the last six months, three out of four Soviet *muftis* had been fired and replaced by tough "Soviet men," ages twenty to thirty, who are considered more "reliable" than the older *ulema*. Mahmud Gekkiev, the *mufti* of the Daghestan, Tolgat Taziev, the *mufti* of Ufa, and Allashukur Pasha Zade, the Shiah *Shaykh ul-Islam* of Transcaucasia, since their nomination have justified the confidence of Moscow by participating very actively in the Soviet propaganda campaign.
- Finally, there is evidence among Soviet Muslims, both believers and non-believers, of a growing confusion between nationalism and religion.

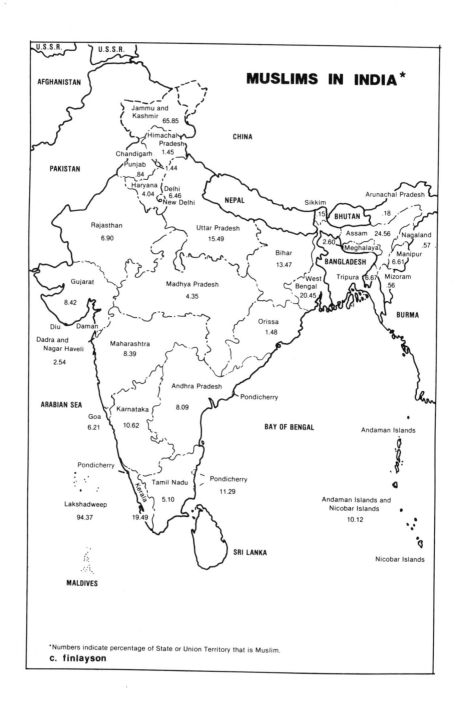

MUSLIMS IN INDIA*

U.S.S.R.
U.S.S.R.
AFGHANISTAN
CHINA

Jammu and
Kashmir 65.85

Himachal
Pradesh 1.45
Chandigarh
Punjab 1.44
.84
Haryana Delhi
4.04 6.46
New Delhi NEPAL

PAKISTAN

Sikkim
.15 BHUTAN
Arunachal Pradesh
.18

Rajasthan
6.90

Uttar Pradesh
15.49

Assam 24.56 Nagaland
2.60 Meghalaya .57
Manipur
6.61

Bihar
13.47

BANGLADESH

Gujarat

8.42

Madhya Pradesh
4.35

West
Bengal
20.45

Tripura 6.67 Mizoram
.56

Diu Daman

Dadra and
Nagar Haveli

2.54

Maharashtra
8.39

Orissa
1.48

BURMA

Andhra Pradesh

Pondicherry

ARABIAN SEA

Goa
6.21

Karnataka
10.62

8.09

BAY OF BENGAL

Andaman Islands

Pondicherry

Lakshadweep

94.37

Kerala

19.49

Tamil Nadu

5.10

Pondicherry
11.29

Andaman Islands and
Nicobar Islands

10.12

SRI LANKA

Nicobar Islands

MALDIVES

*Numbers indicate percentage of State or Union Territory that is Muslim.
c. finlayson

12

Ondia

A CASE STUDY

Walter K. Andersen

HE PARTITION OF BRITISH INDIA IN 1947 produced profound changes in the condition of the Muslim community that remained in India. Muslims, at least at the élite level, had viewed themselves as members of a historic ruling class and were accorded special privileges by the British. Preferential treatment, which had resulted in strong Muslim representation in the civil service, the police and the military, ended in 1947. The system of separate electorates and weighted representation in the legislative bodies was abolished. The Muslim community was reduced from a powerful minority, dominant in several provinces and a quarter of the total population in undivided India, to a mere 10 to 11 percent of the population (see map) and a majority in only nine of India's 365 districts.

The Muslims who remained in India—perhaps 35 million at the time of partition—were not ideologically equipped to cope with a situation in which they were neither the rulers nor the beneficiaries of official privileges. They felt abandoned. The Muslim League, the premier political organization of the community, collapsed. Muslim political leaders shifted en masse to Pakistan, as did a large part of the Muslim police, military personnel, and civil servants. Muslims, moreover, had to bear collective blame for the division of the subcontinent. The recurrent cycles of Indo-Pakistani tension,

The views expressed here are Dr. Andersen's own and not necessarily those of the U.S. Department of State. The author is indebted to Dr. Asad Hussain for many helpful insights.

including three wars, have kept alive doubts concerning the loyalty of Muslims to India. The Muslims thus found themselves with little political leverage and severely reduced representation in the civil service, the military, and the police. They felt discriminated against and alienated from the Indian political system.

Partition also brought in its train the virtual disappearance of the traditional social élites of the Indian Muslim community. Prior to partition, the British and most Muslims recognized the landed aristocrats and a small professional class linked to the aristocrats by family ties as the natural leaders of their community. It was this class that played a dominant role in the Muslim League, which had championed the cause of Pakistan and which had successfully mobilized the great mass of Muslim artisans and peasants between 1937 and 1947. Many left for Pakistan. India's abolition of the landed estates (i.e., *zamindari* abolition) soon after independence greatly undermined what remained of the aristocratic landowning class. A large part of the Muslim population—peasants, artisans, and retainers—thus lost the patronage networks that had given shape to the cultural, social, and political life of the community.

Leadership went, almost by default, to the *ulema*, who were ill-equipped to take the place of the secular aristocratic political élite. The *ulema* in India had no historically legitimate role as political leaders, nor had they had experience in the political arena.

It was not until 1919 that the *ulema* established a political organization, the Jamiat-ul-Ulema-e-Hind, but its focus was primarily pan-Islamic and cultural. It proved unable either to formulate clear political goals or to maintain continuous political activity. It lacked a Mahatma Gandhi or a Muhammad Ali Jinnah, leaders of the Indian National Congress and the Muslim League, respectively, who were able to mold a rational political organization that successfully appealed to deep-seated grievances. The *ulema* generally subscribed to the apolitical notion that the political, economic, and social setbacks of the community resulted from its deviation from the path of true Islam. This message found a popular resonance within the disoriented Muslim community of India during the immediate post-1947 partition period, and such fundamentalist organizations as the Tablighi Jamaat and the Jamaat-e-Islami attracted a substantial following. The ideological blinders of these groups, and others like them, however, rendered the *ulema* incapable of addressing the economic and social problems that lay at the root of the community's grievances.

The changes brought about by partition produced a major reshaping of Muslim demands. Prior to partition, Muslims sought political privileges and were granted preferential treatment on grounds of the community's historical importance and the separateness of its religion and culture.

Following partition, Muslim demands have focused on cultural issues, though Muslims have recently begun to formulate a more inclusive list of distinctly political demands.

Postpartition India is an inhospitable setting for the resuscitation of a religiously-based Muslim political organization. The unwritten ground rules of Indian politics deny legitimacy to political organizations based on religion. This attitude is in large measure a reaction to the successful efforts of the preindependence Muslim League to divide the country. The savage communal riots that rocked the subcontinent during the partition period, and that occur occasionally even now, reinforced the intolerance of the authorities toward religious politics, which are assumed to play a significant role in triggering Hindu-Muslim tensions.

Muslims themselves have remained somewhat aloof from sectarian politics. They apparently have recognized that they can play a meaningful role in the political arena only if they cooperate with other groups or associate with one of the larger secular parties. Muslims are so geographically dispersed that a sectarian party appealing only to Muslims would do poorly at the polls. The high voter turnout of Muslims, on a par with the rest of the population, suggests that most Muslims have accommodated themselves to the existing political order. In addition, the secular orientation of the Indian state, however imperfect in practice, poses no direct threat to Islam. Like many other groups at the lower end of the socioeconomic scale, however, Muslims have run into widespread popular antipathy as they try to assert themselves and aquire a larger share of the economic pie. This problem is less a matter of religion than a struggle among competing groups for limited resources.

India has no official religion, and India's constitution has several provisions that safeguard cultural rights of India's Muslims. Like other religious groups, they can organize and propagate their faith. An effort to legislate restrictions on religious proselytizing aroused a storm of controversy in 1979 and was quietly dropped. A succession of Indian prime ministers, beginning with Jawaharlal Nehru, have made special efforts to assure the Muslim community that its culture and religion are protected.

Indian Muslims live in a country whose dominant religion, Hinduism, is tolerant of religious and cultural deviance. India is so ethnically and socially diverse that it would be surprising if Hinduism were to develop a normative orthodoxy. While there is a Hindu revivalist movement that is suspicious of the "foreign" character of Muslim culture, the relative weakness of this movement reduces the chances that a popular revivalist movement among Muslims will develop to counter it. In fact, the anti-Muslim overtones of Hindu nationalism have diminished considerably, especially since India's relatively easy victory over Pakistan in 1971 and the subsequent creation of the state of Bangladesh.

The Muslims who remained in India after partition understandably adopted a low profile in the political arena. Most of the community looked on the ruling Congress Party as the protector of Muslim interests and, except for a small number of "progressives" who backed the Communists, extended support to it. The Congress Party, for its part, was careful to assert its secular credentials by placing Muslims in highly visible positions of authority. Two Muslims have held the Presidency; two were chief justices of the Supreme Court; several have been state chief ministers. The Janata Party, which held power between 1977 and 1980, similarly placed Muslims in visible positions.

Not until the mid-1960s did Muslims collectively begin to assert themselves in politics. A surge of communal violence in the mid 1960s shocked the community and demonstrated that even the nation's dominant political party could not guarantee communal harmony. Muslim adherence to the Congress Party was shaken. Some urban professionals shifted their support to the Communists and other leftists. Still others considered a separate political forum for Muslims. To this end, the Majlis-e-Mushawarat, a broad confederation of Muslim groups, was established in 1964. Its initial goal was to lobby for Muslim interests. The Mushawarat, however, did not align itself with any party. At the next national elections in 1967, it supported individual candidates who subscribed to a nine-point *Manifesto* that summarized the main grievances and demands of the Muslims.

The nine points were: (1) revision of school textbooks (to eliminate alleged expositions of Hindu customs and beliefs; (2) adoption of a system of proportional representational for legislative bodies (to overcome Muslim underrepresentation); (3) social welfare legislation; (4) removal of government from the personal law of religious groups; (5) use of Urdu as medium of instruction and declaring Urdu the second official language in Uttar Pradesh, Bihar, and other Hindi-speaking states; (6) establishing minority boards to report on welfare of minority communities; (7) maintaining the Muslim character of Aligarh Muslim University; (8) ensuring that religious trusts be reserved for minority members; and (9) removing such "vices" as untouchability, drinking, and risqué literature.

The Mushawarat is most active in the north India states, particularly in Uttar Pradesh and Bihar, the two states which have the largest concentrations of Muslims and which have experienced the most intense communal tension. It decided to run its own candidates after the 1971 elections, but its few successes were registered in constituencies where the organization was allied with large secular party or with other minority groups. Muslim political parties have emerged in a few other places, most prominently in the southwestern state of Kerala, but most Muslims still vote for one of the secular parties.

The increasing assertiveness of the Muslim community created electoral problems for the Congress Party. The Congress in many constituencies rested on a support base of Muslims, Harijans, and upper-caste Hindus. Since Muslims provided the margin of victory in many areas, the loss of their support would result in a major reduction of Congress seats in Parliament and state assemblies. This occurred in the 1967 general elections.

Indira Gandhi was able to win back a substantial part of the Muslim vote in 1971 on a campaign pledge to help the poor. The Congress, however, suffered another erosion of Muslim support in the wake of the 1975-77 State of Emergency. During the Emergency, the government used its vast discretionary power to pursue, *inter alia*, a sterilization campaign and an urban slum removal program. These efforts were most vigorously implemented in areas which coincidentally had large concentrations of Muslims. The outcome was a major shift of Muslim voters to the opposition Janata Party in the 1977 general elections. A resurgence of communal rioting in 1978-79 soured Muslims on the Janata, and they again turned to Gandhi's Congress (Indira) Party in the 1980 general elections.

Communal rioting, which continues, could erode Muslim support for Mrs. Gandhi. It appears, however, that Muslims have tended to blame local law enforcement officials, rather than Gandhi, for the mid-1980 clashes with police. Nevertheless, Muslims have demonstrated that their support cannot be taken for granted. Indeed, their political behavior since the mid-1960s suggests that most important to them are bread-and-butter and law-and-order issues—especially protection against anti-Muslim violence emanating from Hindus.

Besides the economic and social problems which Muslims share with non-Muslims, there are issues that affect Muslims as a group. Muslims are convinced that there is a pattern of discrimination against them. As Dr. Asad Husain observed in his remarks to the conference, "The World of Islam," in Washington in June 1980, the Muslims feel they are considerably worse off than many other Muslim communities in non-Muslim countries—that their situation is deteriorating as a result of Hindu activism.

The depressed socioeconomic condition of Muslims may well account for their low rates of recruitment into civil service, but the persistent demand for an equal opportunity program underscores their belief that they are the victims of a campaign of deliberate discrimination. The low percentage of Muslims in the police, the paramilitary, the army, and the civil service, as well as in educational institutions, is cited as evidence of such discrimination.

There is a precedent for quotas. State governments and the federal government in New Delhi have passed laws setting aside job quotas for

Harijans and other legally defined "backward" Hindu castes on grounds that these groups are victims of historic discrimination. Muslims are now using the same argument, but while there is popular support for continuing the quota system for Harijans and "backward" Hindu castes, there is no comparable backing for applying it to Muslims.

In addition, several cultural issues affect Muslims as a community: minority control of Aligarh Muslim University, an autonomous Muslim Personal Law, and safeguarding the position of the Urdu language. These issues involve symbols of Muslim identification and hence raise questions regarding the integration of Muslims into the national mainstream.

On the one extreme is the view that meeting these cultural demands will encourage Muslim separatism and thus undermine Muslim loyalty to India. This view is most vigorously advanced by Hindu nationalists, but many other Indians, sensitive to the recent division of British India on a communal basis, are similarly apprehensive. In policy terms, this view translates into demands for the cultural assimilation of the Muslim community. The "assimilationists" tend to advance a cultural model whose symbols have their roots in pre-Muslim India and are indisputably Hindu.

The middle position rejects assimilation and argues for a composite culture that blends Muslim and non-Muslim cultural symbols. This view is inscribed in India's Constitution.

At the other extreme is the assertion that the Muslim community is a separate ethnic group. Though the Muslim community is heterogenous, there is a growing willingness on the part of Muslims to accept a common set of cultural symbols and thus to perceive of themselves as a separate ethnic group.

The debate over Urdu dates from the last century. For the greater part of the nineteenth century, Urdu was the dominant official and literary language in northern India and the lingua franca of the whole subcontinent. The Muslim élite, particularly in the United Provinces (now Uttar Pradesh) and Bihar at that time, resisted efforts of an increasingly assertive Hindu urban middle class to displace Urdu with Hindi in the Devanagari script. The debate was closely tied to the political and economic struggle between two sets of competing élites. Hindi was on a par with, if it had not already overtaken, Urdu in much of northern India on the eve of independence. After partition, the status of Urdu plummeted. It was dropped as a language of public instruction. Hindi in the Devanagari script was adopted as the official language of India in the Constitution and the sole official language in Uttar Pradesh, Bihar, and other Hindi-speaking states.

During the subsequent three decades, Urdu supporters have charged that the constitutional rights of Urdu speakers have not been adequately safeguarded. They are right. While state governments are again funding Urdu medium elementary school instruction, most young Muslim students attend non-Urdu medium schools. In many states, including Uttar Pradesh with its huge Muslim population, the government refuses to fund Urdu medium secondary education. Most states, moreover, encourage instruction in the official language of the state by requiring a compulsory paper in that language during the examinations for public service. Bihar is the only state, except for Muslim-majority Kashmir, that has declared Urdu an official language; that was done in 1980 only after the centrally appointed governor issued an ordinance on its behalf. Even that decision met strong opposition in Bihar.

Perhaps no single issue affecting Indian Muslims arouses as much emotion as the question of Muslim personal law (i.e., the *shariah*). Muslims succeeded in convincing the British to exempt Muslim personal law from legislation. They have been similarly successful in independent India, though Article 44 of India's Constitution envisages "a uniform civil code throughout the territory of India" regulating such matters as marriage, divorce, adoption, and inheritance. The government is supposed to prepare the people for the eventual implementation of Article 44, but no Indian government has attempted to do so. A serious effort in this direction would be strongly resisted by the overwhelming majority of India's Muslims.

The emotional Muslim reaction to the personal law issue underscores the widespread belief that adherence to the *shariah* is a religious act comparable to adherence to the injunctions of the Koran and the Sunnah. Even "progressive" Muslims are reluctant to permit government regulation in this field on grounds that the personal law sustains a unique cultural identity. Government law would introduce, it is feared, Hindu or Western practices and thus dilute both religion and culture. These feelings run so deeply that no Indian government is likely in the near future to consider moving toward implementing Article 44.

For over a century, Aligarh Muslim University (AMU) has been a central symbol of Muslim identity in northern India, and simultaneously, a target of Hindu animosity. It was the intellectual hothouse of the Muslim political renaissance and later a center of pro-Pakistani sentiment. Maintaining the "Muslim character" of the University remains a major goal of Indian Muslims.

The British Charter for the University in 1920 gave it a Muslim orientation, and religious instruction was required for all students. After independence the new government moved quickly to dilute the Muslim orientation of the school: a 1951 amendment of the 1920 Charter abolished compulsory religious instruction for non-Muslims, and enhanced the possibility that non-Muslims would serve on the university's governing bodies. Some slight concessions to Muslim demands have been made since that time, but the government is unlikely to grant AMU autonomy. It is concerned that granting autonomy would also establish the unacceptable precedent of a government-funded institution operating outside the government's purview. Nevertheless, most students, administrators, and faculty remain Muslim. The University is still recognized as a major center for the study of Urdu, Persian, and Arabic and of the Muslim states of the pre-British period.

Government policy has been formulated to balance its desire for political integration of the Muslim community, on the one hand, with Muslim demands for the protection of group symbols and for the means (e.g., Urdu schools) to deepen its sense of communal identity and cultural integrity, on the other.

Yet the Muslim community, as Dr. Husain noted at the conference in June, lacks the dynamic, charismatic leadership and the strong political organization that could provide communal cohesion. The élites themselves do not seem well integrated into the Muslim community and are reluctant to speak out against the perceived injustices of the present system and to provide a sense of direction. They will need, in Dr. Husain's view, to begin to take greater interest in the situation of the community in India and in the trend toward greater activism that is increasingly apparent in the world of Islam outside India. At the same time, Indian Muslims are encouraged by the attention they are receiving from their fellow Muslims in other states and are determined to survive as a community in India and to help shape India's destiny, as well as to participate in the revival of Islam globally.

Part 3

Cultural Diversity and Religious Unity

ISLAM PROVIDES NOT ONLY A SIMPLE, DIRECT, and comprehensive central core of belief, but also an extensive, all-inclusive body of instruction about how the believer should think, live, and act. The often heard description of Islam as a way of life is quite literally true.

The Prophet Muhammad received the Koran in Arabic and, during his lifetime, delivered the new message to his own people—Arabs living relatively simple lives as herdsmen and traders on the Red Sea cost of Arabia. From the Muslim community in Medina, dating from 622, the faith spread rapidly throughout Arabia.

In the first years after the Prophet's death, Arab armies carried the new faith with eruptive force across North Africa and into Spain, and eastward into Persia. Thereafter, Islam was brought more slowly into India, Central Asia, and Africa by Arabs and others through conquest, trade, and missionary effort.

During several periods of expansion, the Muslims overran large areas of the world, some of which had civilizations of antiquity and sociocultural systems that were both complex and sophisticated. The Koran enjoined Muslims to tolerate the monotheists (Christians and Jews)—"People of the Book"—whom they found in these conquered countries, but to convert the polytheists and to slay those who resisted Islam. The predictable result was large-scale conversion of pagans.

There is no reason to doubt that to the great majority of the converts in the first or second generation after the Prophet, the monotheistic and vibrant message of Islam was welcome and sincerely accepted, or that such tenets as the equality of man in the sight of God met with much real resistance. On the other hand, previous patterns were not entirely uprooted or superceded. Instead, there was continuous interaction between Islam and pre-existing cultures. The results were new syntheses and combinations over time that led to a range of Islamic societies, united in the essentials of Islam but revealing diverse ways of facing and attempting to solve the problems which life presents.

Examples of this cultural diversity and religious unity run through the four essays in this section. The first discusses Islam in Saudi Arabia, where it was born. The second examines Islam in West Africa, to which it came relatively late. The third essay deals with Islam in Turkey, the successor to the Ottoman Empire and for centuries the "Sword of Islam," which might have been expected for that reason to be a religion-based nation but which is one of the few officially secular states in the Muslim world. And the fourth summarizes the present role of Islam in Indonesia, the world's largest Muslim country.

13

Saudi Arabia

ISLAMIC TRADITIONALISM AND MODERNIZATION

Malcolm C. Peck

S AUDI ARABIA IS AT ONCE THE MOST MUSLIM AND THE MOST ARAB of countries. Its traditional, ethnoreligious homogeneity, however, has included significant social and cultural diversity. Foreign forces of economic modernization now challenge the values on which Saudi society and government have rested at the center of the Arab and Islamic worlds.

The origins of contemporary Saudi Arabia in central Arabia in the eighteenth century reflect both the tribal and Islamic sources of its legitimacy. Muhammad ibn Saud, founder of the Saudi dynasty, was ruler of the town of Diriya and came from the Anaza tribe which enjoys "sharif" or noble status among Arabian tribes. To this was added the more consequential legitimating force of religion, when ibn Saud granted protection in 1744 to an Islamic reformer named Muhammad ibn Abdul-Wahhab, who had won the enmity of other local rulers through his religious teachings against laxity and corruption in the practice of Islam.

Abdul-Wahhab was a Muslim fundamentalist of the strict constructionist Hanbali school of Islamic law. He preached a return to the original purity of Islam, unencumbered by subsequent accretions of interpretation and practice, with emphasis on the absolute oneness of God. For this reason, the followers of his teachings are properly called *muwahhidun*, though more commonly they are referred to as Wahhabis. (The influence of Abdul-Wahhab on the spiritual orientation of the kingdom can be seen in the prominent role his descendants play in the various religious ministries and is reflected in their final name, the "ash shaykh.") Ibn Saud and Abdul-Wahhab formed a compact of sword and faith that enabled the ruler to extend his sway rapidly over the Najd, the heartland of Arabia. By the early nineteenth century, Saudi forces, welded together from tribes loyal to the Saud family and animated by the force of crusading religious reform (and sometimes by the prospect of booty) had conquered most of the Arabian Peninsula.

The process was in large degree duplicated by King Abdul-Aziz ibn Saud when he restored the family's fortunes in the twentieth century. In both instances, the Saudi embodiment of Arab Bedouin values and reformist Islam combined to provide the rulers with a dynamic legitimizing force that proved irresistible. A further, highly significant dimension of legitimacy derived from the fact that no colonial power had ever controlled Saudi territory nor played a direct role in the establishment of the Saudi regime.

The restoration began with a daring raid led by the young Abdul-Aziz against Riyadh in January 1902. This was the first step in the recovery of his ancestral kingdom, lost largely through internal rivalries to the Sauds' rival clan in the Najd, the Rashids. A decade later Abdul-Aziz revealed his innovative brilliance in establishing the Ikhwan ("brethren"), which served to conjoin, as his ancestor Muhammad ibn Saud had done, Arab tribal energies and the all-embracing power of Wahhabi Islam. The Ikhwan's settled communities of Najdi warriors promoted agriculture and provided the zealous soldiery which reconquered the Saudi patrimony. By 1921 the Rashids were defeated, and by 1926 the Hashemite presence in the Hejaz had been eliminated.

The latter event brought Abdul-Aziz a new and important position in the international Islamic community: he became guardian of the Holy Places in Mecca and Medina. It also added to the kingdom (which was named Saudi Arabia in 1932) a province, the Hejaz, with a very different population and culture than the Najd. The annual pilgrimage (*hajj*) and a well-established merchant trade with the outside world had given the Hejaz a more cosmopolitan and heterogeneous character than central Arabia or the other parts of the expanded kingdom.

The pragmatic accommodations which Abdul-Aziz was obliged to make in governing the Hejaz and in meeting his international responsibilities to the whole Muslim community, as well as in dealing with British power, which he now encountered on his new northern border and in the Gulf, led to a break with the Ikhwan. Several of his principal lieutenants, who bridled at negotiating and compromising with non-Muslim powers and at tolerating Muslim practices at odds with their form of Islam, rebelled against the King. After crushing their revolt he exercised traditional Arab generosity in bringing the former rebels back to the fold. But the revolt of the Ikhwan foreshadowed problems which would reemerge as the traditional values and practices that sustained the Saudi polity were confronted by the intrusions of the outside world.

His accommodation with new realities did not mean that Abdul-Aziz had abandoned his commitment to Wahhabi Islam. Wahhabism continued to be the kingdom's ideological foundation. Acknowledgement of the Koran and the other sources of the *shariah* as the nation's constitution was a shrewd way in which to confirm Islamic legitimacy, and to leave open specific questions about how to deal with contemporary issues which were unanticipated by the early Muslim community. Abdul-Aziz, himself learned in the *shariah*, was careful to justify each new departure—technological, political or other—in terms of what was permitted by Islam and to secure the assent of the *ulema* at each step. Thus the fateful embrace of the process of modernization was accomplished without rejecting or even ostensibly diluting the country's fundamentalist Islamic character.

After World War II, the kingdom began to earn oil revenues in significant quantity, and the first large influx of Americans and other foreigners with technical and managerial skills commenced. The socioeconomic system that had evolved through the centuries on the basis of an ecology of scarcity now faced the beginning of its end. The thirst of a rebuilding Europe pushed income from oil upward (though not so dramatically as in the 1970s) as the King's long reign came to an end in 1953. The process of modernization was launched, but its implications were not yet fully discerned. A modern political or administrative structure had barely begun to emerge with the old King's ad hoc approach to meeting new problems. The portentous challenge of holding together the kingdom in a hostile world of multiple challenges fell to Saud, the eldest son of King Abdul-Aziz.

Saud, while possessing some of the traditional Bedouin virtues, lacked his father's capacity for leadership. He was unequal to the task of guiding a state which was caught up in a process of profound transformation and which faced a circle of hostile neighbors. His profligate spending of oil revenues brought near bankruptcy amidst affluence, and did much to discredit him in the royal and religious establishments. Further, his incautious external policy toward Nasser and other radical Arab leaders, then posing a major threat to Saudi Arabia, helped lead to a de facto transfer of power to his brother Faisal in 1958, and to the latter's formal accession as king in 1964.

The deposition of Saud offers an illuminating example of how Saudi Arabia's traditional Arab-Islamic establishment can cope with a major state crisis, and it also suggests the inaccuracy of the epithet "absolute" that the western press commonly applied to the Saudi monarchy. The leading princes of the Saud family and the principal members of the *ulema* form "the people who loose and bind." This group determined Saud's unfitness, imposed his deposition and asked Faisal to assume his place. A *fatwa* or formal legal opinion of the religious court confirmed Faisal's accession. In this way was manifest both the constraining and supporting role of Islam.

Faisal assumed his responsibilities with a combination of qualities that ideally suited him to rule. He was deeply religious by nature and training—at least in part because he was a direct descendant on his mother's side of Muhammad ibn Abdul-Wahhab. Moreover, from early youth, he had proved himself in important diplomatic missions, military campaigns, and administrative duties. As a ruler of respected piety and astute political sense, he was commited both to preserving Islamic values in Saudi Arabia while advancing them elsewhere, and to promoting the modernization of his country. It was a measure of his statesmanship that he was able to reconcile these divergent aims during his reign.

Faisal's modest, even austere, style of rule and personal religious devotion contrasted sharply with Saud's profligacy and helped confirm the pervasive strength of Wahhabi Muslim norms. Promotion of religious values extended beyond national borders. Not only were immediate, smaller neighbors pressured to conform to more conservative Mulsim practices, but also a major effort was devoted to international activity to advance solidarity among Muslim states and to promote their spiritual and material well-being. Thus a series of Islamic Summit Conferences and a separate series of annual Islamic Foreign Ministers Conferences were inaugurated to coordinate national policies with the aim of furthering Muslim goals. The permanent Islamic Conference organization, in some measure, has met its aim of helping to resolve controversies among Muslim states, and the generous foreign assistance program that Faisal established is aimed principally at the Arab and Muslim worlds. These efforts, in part, were intended to blunt the threat of radical Arab nationalism, but they were also genuine expressions of the King's view of the world, based on classical Islamic formulations. Faisal's dramatic move to impose an oil embargo against the US in October 1973, following what he perceived to be the lack of American evenhandedness toward the Arab-Israeli conflict, was an assertion of new-found Arab-Islamic strength.

Nevertheless, Faisal's commitment to the rapid modernization of Saudi Arabia's economy and the accelerated internal transformation and the expanded contacts with non-Muslim cultures that followed posed a redoubtable challenge to the Islamic core values of Saudi society. During his reign the creation of a modern administrative bureaucracy began in earnest. The *ulema* became part of the bureaucracy, and such functions as education, which had been traditionally within the purview of the religious establishment, were partly removed from it. Moreover, capable young Saudis, as career opportunities multiplied, were less drawn to careers as men of religion. The infrastructural and industrial projects begun under Faisal brought greatly increased numbers of non-Muslims into the kingdom, and engendered an augmented flow of young Saudis overseas for training in Western educational institutions, which inevitably involved exposure to secular values. While these students and their society appeared to hold fast to the values that had created and sustained Saudi Arabia, it could be asked at Faisal's death in 1975 whether his remarkable achievement of bringing his country into an affluent and troubled present while preserving its special Arab-Islamic legacy could be sustained.

In considering the scope of the challenge to contemporary Saudi Arabia it is well to look briefly at the dimensions of the change which it is now undergoing. Little more than a generation ago, per capita annual income in Saudi Arabia was one of the lowest in the world; today it stands upwards of $25,000. Just over two decades ago there were no public schools for girls; today most school-age girls are being educated. Only a few years ago most Saudis lived in small towns and villages and many were nomads; now the majority lives in large cities, and the true Bedouins largely have disappeared. Two vast industrial complexes are being built, at Yanbu on the Red Sea and Jubayl on the Gulf, which will be peopled overnight with tens of thousands of transplanted Saudis. Meanwhile, the commitment to rapid industrialization brings ever more foreigners—many of them Palestinians and other non-Saudi Arabs—into the kingdom to undertake tasks which Saudis are not yet equipped or disposed to perform. Despite the vast expansion of the kingdom's university system, thousands of Saudis continue to study in foreign, principally American, institutions.

Saudi Arabians might be said to be suffering from "future shock." Profound questions are raised in Saudi Arabia about whether the headlong pace of modernization is necessary or wise, whether the end result of the transformation will bear resemblance to the familiar and comforting world of the past, and whether the spiritual and other traditional qualities that have rendered life meaningful—even if circumscribed—will be compromised or lost in return for uncertain material and intellectual gains. For many Saudis, these gains may seem questionable and the losses in human, moral, and cultural terms greatly excessive.

Posing these questions, however, does not presuppose pessimistic answers. Indeed, the influence of secularism and materialism has not necessarily become ascendant. The basic value of close ties among all members of the extended family and of collective responsibility for the actions of one of its members remains intact. Islam, as it regulates Saudi life through the *shariah* courts and other formal institutions and as it affects Saudis in innumerable subtle and informal ways, is still very much alive. The annual *hajj* now involves some two million pilgrims, Saudi and foreign, and the issue of sovereignty over East Jerusalem and its Muslim shrines, second in importance for Sunni Muslims only to those of Mecca and Medina, is an issue on which the Saudi government feels most strongly. Moreover, the executions of the young prince who assassinated King Faisal and of the princess of the sensationalized "Death of a Princess' docu-drama served to remind everyone that the laws of Islam apply to members of the royal family as well as to all others who transgress them. Summary justice was also meted out to those who committed sacrilege by their attack on the Grand Mosque in November 1979.

These episodes, however, and especially the last, are symptomatic of the social and cultural strains caused by the impact of unsettling change on a traditional society. Despite the royal family's Islamic legitimacy, the attempted insurrection in Mecca was apparently engendered principally by Muslim fundamentalists who were convinced that the course and pace of development were leading Saudis away from Islam. While this manifestation of a challenge from the religious caught by Saudis by surprise, one prescient observer, Michael C. Hudson, in *Arab Politics*, had noted the danger in advance: "Although destroyed as an organized force, it is well to remember that the Ikhwan represented a deep current of legitimacy in Saudi political culture, and that the family was vulnerable to attack from the religious right wing before as well as after the onset of oil wealth and social modernization" (p.173).

The attack also appears to have had tribal and political motivation, and thus suggests other areas of danger as well. Despite the considerable degree of cultural homogeneity enjoyed by Saudi Arabia, regional diversity, generation gaps, and socioeconomic disparities point to potential cleavages. These, exacerbated by the massive influx of foreigners, Arab and non-Arab, threaten to undo the largely successful integrating effort of over half a century.

A particularly sensitive area of threat derives from the one instance where real integration within the kingdom has not taken place—the shiah community in Eastern (Hasa) Province. Here, the perception of Saudi mistreatment, the key role of shiahs in the oil industry and general economy of the province, and the appeal of Ayatollah Khomeini's incendiary sermons from across the Gulf are a dangerous mixture. Serious rioting by large numbers of Shiah has already occurred.

The question has been raised whether Khomeini and the Iranian revolution may find resonance in Saudi Arabia. The answer probably is negative, given the kingdom's intensely sunni legacy, the intertwining of the political and religious establishments, and the other features which make Saudi Arabia and Iran (before or after the revolution) so dissimilar. But Khomeini's message gives added and disturbing force to the questions noted above that are directed with ever greater insistence to the process of modernization and its social and cultural costs.

The Saudi leadership seems to have concluded that the commitment to rapid economic-industrial development should be maintained, despite its risks. Long-range prosperity presumably will depend on the transformation of oil export earnings into more enduring forms of income-generating wealth during the few decades remaining in the petroleum age. It may well be also that a slow-down in the provision of the goods and services the Saudis expect would cause much more sociopolitical trauma than a continued and augmented flow. The enormous challenge, then, is to accommodate far-reaching social changes, while keeping the essential core of Arab-Islamic tradition vital and relevant. To be optimistic, one may suggest that Islamic values, and religious values generally, are not necessarily the impediment to modern nation-building that many Western social scientists have supposed, and indeed, in some cases, may be facilitators of change. If the royal family successfully can project its commitment to the religious-cultural values that gave birth to its rule, if the old informal egalitarianism of the *majlis* can dominate emerging political institutions, and if regional and international crises do not engulf the kingdom, then it is likely that the challenge will be met.

The author is indebted to John Duke Anthony and R. Bayly Winder for their contributions to this chapter.

14

Sub-Saharan Africa

ISLAMIC PENETRATION

Sulayman S. Nyang

𝓣HE ADVENT OF ISLAM IN AFRICA was a result of the rapid sweep of the Muslim armies in the early decades of the Islamic movement. Although Africans had contacts with Arabians prior to the rise of Islam, Africa's territorial integrity and the destiny of its people were not threatened by Arabians until Egypt fell into their hands in the seventh century.

Thereafter, the Arab armies (Egyptians and Berbers) began to search for new kingdoms and new opportunities. Those who came as military governors founded towns and villages that later became the basis of urban life and culture in the northern part of Africa.

The conquest of the Maghrib—the western part of *Dar ul-Islam* (the world of Islam)—gave rise to two processes: Arabization and Islamization. The first process proved successful because Arabic was the language of government and trade. As the language of the conquerors from the East, its prestige and usefulness enabled it gradually to gain ground.

A major factor assisting in the realization of the process of Islamization was the mercantile community. The merchants, who came from as far away as Persia to conduct business, were bent on gaining a foothold in the centers of civilization in the Maghrib. It was in this role, therefore, that they made a meaningful contribution to the Islamization of this region of Africa. Indeed, the intermingling of peoples and cultures paved the way for the gradual penetration of Islam in the Maghrib.

By the eleventh century the predominantly Berber people of the Maghrib, now Muslim and Arabized, had brought Islam across the Sahara and into the sub-Saharan region. With the religion came the changes in institutions and values which derive from it. Basic among these were beliefs that conflicted with and overrode preexisting African tenets.

Islamic theology sees man as a privileged creature to whom God has given trust on earth; that is to say, man is called upon to serve as God's vice-regent on earth and to account for each of his deeds in this sublunary world. In the Islamic belief system, it is taught that, although life is short and full of evil, man should take heart for there is life beyond the grave.

One could argue that the Islamic view of man sees him as a creature whose identity is determined both by himself and by God. The Koran addresses numerous warnings to rebellious mankind not to go astray; it also announces that, in the last days of the earth, God surely will bring to justice all those who have taken no note of man's finitude, his dependency and his judgment before God.

The promise of a hereafter is a major difference between Islam and traditional African thought, which generally pays less attention to the details of a hereafter. The traditional African cosmologist focuses primarily on man's post-mortem relations with his family, his clan, his tribe, and those who have survived him. One could say that old Africa believed that immortality was obtained through the acts of respect shown to departed ancestors by the community of the living, or through the gradual recession of the dead ancestor into the realm of the spirits. The expansion of Islam in Africa, therefore, had great significance for the peoples of the continent.

Islam came to Africa as a belief system that prided itself on its command of the written word and on the material culture associated with the *Word of Allah*. As a result, it is not surprising that its propagators found it necessary to teach their doctrines and rituals while trading with the inhabitants of African kingdoms in or south of the Sahel. This economic intercourse between the Arabs and the Berbers, on the one hand, and Black Africans to the south, on the other, opened the door to greater cultural penetration.

When we look at the balance sheet of Arabo-Islamic/African relations, we find that the major contribution of Islam in the continent is in the realm of intellectual, social, and cultural development.

On the intellectual plane, Islam introduced a new way of looking at life, man, and community. Previously the African lived in a self-contained world that restricted his cultural and mental encounters to the ecological setting of his primary ethnic group. The impact of Islam on his consciousness, however, gave rise to a sense of cosmopolitanism; this fact was not lost on the first Europeans to set foot on Muslim lands in West Africa. The conversion of the tribal African exposed him for the first time to the brotherhood of Islam whose borders were beyond what he could see and whose message was directed to everyone living on this planet.

On the social plane, the conversion of the tribal African to Islam offered the possibility of interethnic cooperation. That the Muslim propagators were usually merchants made the converts more receptive to the new ideas and the new wares their coreligionists brought into their areas. Even if the trade were between non-Muslims and Muslims, the relationships exposed the non-Muslims to Islamic modes of trade and commerce. Islam thus provided a common moral basis for commerce and trade, and the *shariah* guided the Muslim merchants in their dealing with one another and with their non-Muslim customers.

The link between trade and Islam made it possible for the convert gradually to develop a degree of trust and confidence in men who did not necessarily speak his language but who embraced the teachings of his newly adopted religion. This new attitude toward non-members of the ethnic group was revolutionary, and its potential for enhanced interethnic communication was of great significance. Though Islam was not primarily responsible for the founding of the three great West African empires (Ghana, Mali and Songhai), these empires and their rulers profited from the Islamic symbols of their day. Their cultural and economic systems, moreover, in varying degrees were exposed to the forces and pressures of the Islamic centers of civilization far to the north and northeast.

In dealing with the Islamic contribution to the social universe of Africans, it can be argued that the arrival of Islam widened the horizons of traditional Africans. Whereas in the past this African trusted his destiny to the spirits who resided in a well, a tree, or a stream in the ecological setting of his tribal group, and whereas he wished to placate the gods and his ancestors, under Islam he discovered that his life was for an appointed time and that his deeds on earth had a singular meaning. He also learned from his Islamic mentors that he would be held accountable in the hereafter for whatever he did in his lifetime. The only way he could save his soul and himself on the Day of Judgment was to accept the responsibility of living. In other words, the conversion of the traditional African meant the gradual realization on his part of the spiritual loneliness of man in the world and his responsibility to live up to the expectations of his religion.

This understanding of self and of life led many African converts to try to put into practice the rituals and teaching of Islam. It is in their attempt to live up to the Islamic ideal that many traditional Africans learned to pray with fellow Muslims or to stand alone before Allah. In their desire to win the favors of their Maker, they learned to fulfill the expectations of the Koran's teachings with respect to cleanliness and modesty in clothing.

Writing on what Islam meant to African converts some years before the European powers divided up the greater part of the African continent, R. Bosworth Smith, in his *Mohammedanism in Africa* (1887), identified areas of the African social universe in which Islam was establishing its influence. He noted that the adoption of Islam by traditional Africans increased their understanding of hygiene and made them aware that the covering of one's physical nakedness was a great step toward the covering of one's spiritual nakedness before Allah. Smith also pointed out that the arrival of Islam in West Africa broadened the basis of social solidarity which in turn led to the formation of supertribal or imperial political organizations. The growth of political consciousness among Muslims of diverse ethnic background, in Smith's view, was largely a result of the sense of community created by Islam. He also believed that Islam had a great impact on traditional African society because it ushered in a revolution in the mental estate of the individual. He sums up his view of the Islamic impact this way: "As regards the individual, it is admitted on all hands that Islam gives to its new Negro converts an energy, a dignity, a self-reliance, and a self-respect which is all too rarely found in their Pagan or their Christian fellow countrymen."

On the cultural plane, the advent of Islam meant a great deal to many African societies. If we identify the material, value, and institutional bases of a society as the essential aspects of its culture, we can then demonstrate the manner in which Islam affected the cultural realm of traditional Africans.

The advent of Islam in the Sahelian areas in the medieval period led to the penetration of the region by Arab and Berber merchants. The trade and commercial ties between the states in the Maghrib and their sisters to the East, on the one hand, and the Black African kingdoms to the south of the Sahara, on the other, led to the slave raids and the slave trade across the Sahara. This trade depleted the kingdoms in the forest belts of thousands of human beings who were forced to leave their homes, never to return, but it also laid the foundation for the Arab and Berber invasion of Ghana in 1076. Indeed, the trade and commerce between the Arabo-Berber states to the north and the sub-Saharan states was a cause of the depopulation of African kingdoms below the Sahel. There is also evidence that the colonization of the continent by Europeans was partly motivated by their desire to wrest power and trade routes from their Muslim rivals. Further, in this context, Africa's woes and wounds were the products of Arabo-Berber greed for gold and slaves. But the physical and psychological injuries could also be attributed to the treachery of some of sub-Saharan Africa's own children whose greed and ruthlessness revealed their baser instincts.

Islam was not really the motive force behind such atrocities. Like Christianity in later years, Islam served as an instrument of rationalization. Viewed from this perspective, Europe's "discovery" and subsequent colonization of Africa were the result of the frantic efforts of Europeans who wanted to weaken Islamic power in the name of Christianity and to establish imperial preserves to glorify their newly fashioned nationalisms. Though some aggressive European nationalists might have seen Christianity as a horse that could transport them to the "Dark Continent" where they could play out their self-appointed rule of cosmic transformers, the Christian horse was very reluctant to follow the riders' command. In saying this, however, we must concede that the colonial power tended to treat this religious horse as a Trojan horse sent from Europe to Africa. As a result of the nationalistic and political usages to which it was put, many Africans came to see Christianity as a tool in Caesar's service.

At the institutional level, Islam introduced many changes in African life. The arrival of a Muslim scholar in an African community often led to the establishment of a *madrasah* (Koranic school). This new institution gradually replaced, or coexisted with, the traditional centers of education, and the students who were brought before the Koranic teacher were slowly inducted into the Islamic culture of the north and northeast.

Besides the Koranic school, there were other forms of cultural borrowing. As it gradually penetrated African consciousness, Islam began to invade the African conceptual world. Soon the process of linguistic imbibition started to take effect. Consciously or unconsciously, newly converted African Muslims began to abandon traditional words in their languages in favor of borrowed Islamic terminology.

Another example of institutional borrowing were the *tariqat* (sufi brotherhoods). As Nehemia Levtzion correctly points out, these brotherhoods became significant in the Sahel in the eighteenth and nineteenth centuries. The arrival of the Sufi brotherhoods ushered in a train of developments that affected the history of many African societies south of the Sahara. As is noted in the growing literature on the Islamic *jihads* (holy wars) in the Sahel, the followers of the Sufi brotherhoods played an important role. Some of these *jihad* warriors (*mujahidin*) felt that it was their religious duty to purge Islam of decadence and corruption. For this reason they were willing to wage war against those they perceived as vile *ulema*.

In light of these developments, it seems clear that the sufi brotherhoods in the Sahel contributed significantly to the growth of Muslim solidarity and cohesiveness at the élite level. In fact, the growing immersion of African Muslims in Islamic culture, together with their desire to play a more active role in the political systems of their times, may have led many of the élites to agitate for reform and change in the lives of their non-Muslim peoples.

Finally, there is the use of Arabic script for reducing African languages to writing. This Arabo-Islamic cultural contribution is significant because it led to the emergence of a limited form of literacy among many of the Muslim peoples of the Sahel. The first products of this new technology of intellectual conservation were the epistles and explanatory comments written down by the *ulema*.

Regardless of the limitations of this new technology, there is strong evidence that it had a major impact on the social universe of traditional Africans. Edward Blyden, the celebrated black intellectual, was much impressed by the influence of Islam on the black man. He and some of his Christian contemporaries thought that the advance of Islam was a prologue to the real drama—the eventual Christianization of Africans. Blyden, in his attempt to demonstrate the cultural impact of Islam in *Christianity, Islam and the Negro Race*, quoted Barth as saying that some of the vernaculars had been enriched by Arabic expressions "for the embodiment of the higher processes of thought." He added that, "they have received terms regarding the religion of one God, and respecting a certain state of civilization, such as marrying, reading, writing . . . and phrases of salutation and of good breeding; then came the terms relating to dress, instruments, and the art of warfare as well as architecture [and] commerce" (p. 187).

In summary, the African consciousness today is bordered by three forces that are competing for primacy: the traditional African culture that predates the arrival of Islam, the Islamic element, and what the African calls the Euro-Western element.

When we talk about the Islamic experience in Africa, we have to bear in mind that toward the end of the nineteenth century a new phenomenon—Western colonialism—manifested itself in the region. Western colonialism had a great impact on African consciousness. It affected the material base, the institutional base, the value base of African society. Today, when we talk about Islam in the region we have to remember that Islam coexists with two other cultural systems and that Africans are trying to work out a synthesis.

We Africans find ourselves in the same position as Thomas Aquinas and others who were trying to reconcile three elements in European consciousness: pagan Rome, Israel, and Hellenic Greece. We have to reconcile the Islamic, the traditional African, and the Euro-Western legacies.

15

Islam in Turkey

Talat Sait Halman

HE TURKISH NATION should become even more religious—more religious in all the purity of faith." Mustafa Kemal Pasha made this statement in February 1924, a few months after proclaiming the Turkish Republic, which in the following years would pursue the policy of making education and public administration secular. The reforms introduced by Mustafa Kemal Pasha (later Ataturk) were to constitute the most extensive secularization ever undertaken by a Muslim nation: with lightning speed, government and education were divorced from Islam, the legal system Europeanized, the Caliphate abolished, the Arabic script (sacrosanct orthography of the Koran) replaced by the Latin alphabet, many symbols of tradition removed (the fez outlawed and the veil forced out), and virtually all religious institutions as well as the religious brotherhoods stamped out by fiat.

The thrust of Ataturk's "New Turkey" was toward modernity patterned after European models. It sought to remove the monolithic Islamic faith which, for a millennium, had given the Turks—the Seljuks and the Ottomans—their *spiritus movens* and most of the dominant components of their culture. Witna a few years, in his opening address at the Grand National Assembly's new session in late 1932, Ataturk was able to announce: "We are by now a Western nation."

The secularist reforms, bold and difficult as they were, derived some of their imperatives from Turkish history and culture: Turks encountered Islam in their nomadic period. In a sense, they became, and remained, the "dark horses of Islam." Although they absorbed Islamic culture, they probably retained, in their collective consciousness the Jungian archetypes of nomadism. Islam was superimposed on their own personality—the hodja's robe placed on the horseman. As the Turkologist Barthold once observed: "The Turk is nothing if not a nomad." The observation holds a large measure of truth because it brings out the adoptive and adaptive aspects of mobility, not only in terms of movement through space and climate but also the receptiveness to change. Without belaboring the point, it may be argued that Islam, for the Turk, was not an artificial but a somewhat superficial phenomenon. Even at the zenith of the Ottoman Empire, with its unswerving dedication to the glory of Islam, the Turks had many autochthonous cultural dimensions unrelated to their acquired faith. Even if they held Islam's most sacred cities, they were essentially outsiders, away from Islam's spiritual and cultural inner sanctum.

Characteristically, the Ottoman state, although essentially theocratic, maintained in practical and pragmatic terms a separation of religion from the governmental process. The "Islamic" establishment remained in charge of doctrine, of education, of social and intellectual life, particularly in the urban areas. The ruling establishment, the patron and protector of Islam and the *shariah*, controlled all temporal power. The separation grew from the early nineteenth century onward as a result of political, technological and legal reforms, while the Ottoman state struggled to rescue itself from collapse.

In the era of decline, the Ottoman religious institutions had become ossified and anachronistic. The so-called "doctors of law" appeared to nineteenth century intellectuals as proctors of vested interest. Religious leaders of the past were blamed for having blocked innovation and progress—a fact dramatized by their ability to delay the establishment of the printing press until the late 1720s. During the decades of Ottoman twilight, there was growing awareness that the tightly shut "gates of interpretation" (*ijtihad*) had imposed isolation and barrenness on intellectual life.

Although the Ottomans represented the epicenter and the epic sweep of Islam and were the political masters of its domain for more than 400 years, they had been its cultural slaves for 600 years. Ottoman imperialism viewed Islam as an ideology binding the brethren together. The fervor of Arab nationalism came as a rude awakening. All the efforts to strengthen Islamic solidarity in the closing years of the Ottoman state met with dismal failure. Pan-Islamism did not work. To add insult to injury, many Arab writers (e.g., Rifaa Rafi al-Tahtawi) were accusing "barbarian Turks" of "the devastation of Arab civilization." The Ottoman Sultan's call in 1914 for *jihad* (holy war) to unite all Muslims turned out to be a fiasco. The Caliphate, held by the Ottoman dynasty since the early sixteenth century, had clearly become a liability in the early twentieth century.

Progressively, from the latter part of the nineteenth century onward, many Ottoman intellectuals came to regard religion itself as a deterrent to socioeconomic change. In retrospect, they realized the fallacy, the vicious cycle, perpetrated by some of the best minds of the past: in two major memoranda given to two sultans, in 1631 and 1640 respectively, Koci Bey, to cite a glaring example, had brilliantly diagnosed the ailments of the system, yet, as panacea, he had emphatically recommended the strengthening of Islam's traditional values. Even the late nineteenth century compromise formula, which roughly corresponded to "Ex Oriente lux, ex Occidente frux," seemed suspect: many intellectuals did not trust the "spiritual light of the East," because it was inextricably intertwined with the theocratic, monarchic, static, and tyrannical system. There were also occasional attacks on religion: the most influential Turkish poet at the turn of the century, Tevfik Fikret, wrote a long poem entitled "Tarih-i Kadim" (Ancient History) in 1905, which includes the following couplet: "Faith craves martyrs, heaven wants sacrifice: / Everywhere, all the time, blood, blood, blood." He and some of his contemporaries introduced new concepts of rationalism, scientific inquiry, empirical positivism, etc.

From the time he started the national liberation struggle in 1919 to the proclamation of the Republic in 1923, Mustafa Kemal Pasha did not give any inkling of an anti-religious predilection. On the contrary, he maintained effective relations with many religious leaders, including the sheikhs of various sects, most of whom supported the war effort on the assumption that the Caliphate might be saved. Although there are no records of him performing the ritual prayers (*namaz*), many photographs of the late 1910s and early 1920s depict him reciting prayers, with hands opened upward in the traditional way, in public. On the rostrum of the National Assembly, which convened in 1920, stood a copy of the Koran and the "Sakal-i Serif" (blessed hairs from the Prophet's beard). Many of the sentiments expressed in the new national anthem's words (written in 1921 by the devout patriotic poet and Member of Parliament Mehmet Akif, who was to leave Turkey in 1925 because of his opposition to the secular reforms) were ardently religious. Mustafa Kemal Pasha himself made effective use of Islamic values and symbols. Significantly, he was known, popularly as well as officially, as "Gazi" (from the Arabic "ghazi," meaning heroic warrior in the cause of Islam).

It was in the months preceding the establishment of the Republic in October 1923 that the national leader, having decided not to start a dynasty of his own and probably already planning to abolish the Caliphate, made several statements which, although full of respect, emphasized the need to reconcile Islamic tenets and practices with the requirements of modern life and to interpret them in terms of rationalism:

> Our religion is the most rational and naturalistic faith. It is as a consequence of this that it became the last religion. For religious faith to be authentic, it must conform to the intellect—to science, scholarship, and logic. Our religion is consonant with all these.
>
> Our religion does not recommend lowliness, lethargy or humiliation to our nation. On the contrary, both Allah and the Prophet command that human beings and nations should uphold their dignity and honor.

The Gazi's republic, less than 100 days after coming into existence, abolished the Caliphate, expelled from Turkey all members of the Ottoman dynasty, and liquidated the Ministry of Islamic Law and Pious Foundations. Revolutionary measures followed in quick succession—closing of the congregation places and the mausolea of the Islamic brotherhoods, the introduction of secular education, replacement of the legal system with the adapted versions of the Swiss Civil Code, German Business Law, and Italian Penal Code. In 1928, Article 2 of the Turkish Constitution—"The Moslem religion is the religion of the Turkish nation"—was removed by an act of Parliament. Later in that year, the language reform abruptly changed the Turkish writing system from the Arabic alphabet to the Latin for the purpose, inter alia, of cutting off the new generations from the Islamic Ottoman past with its Arabo-Persian orientation, along with other reforms designed to guide Turkey into modernity in the European mode.

Secularism mobilized itself against some immediate and critical targets: It sought to do away with the old regime, with the lingering "sanctity" of the Sultanate, with the recalcitrance of the conservative religious establishment that was potentially a seditious force as demonstrated by scattered incidents including Kurdish uprisings. Turkey was also anxious to dissociate itself from the burdens which the rest of the Muslim world might have imposed on it through the Caliphate.

The secularist thrust, however, had a grand design, and constituted an ambitious strategy for revolutionary transformation. It went far beyond, in its ideals, the goal of removing tired old values and institutions or of sparing the budding minds from reactionary homiletics and Arabic catechisms. It was not merely a means of accelerating the transition from a theocratic system to a modernizing nation-state. The sweeping change Ataturk and his colleagues sought to achieve in all sectors—politics, economy, justice, education, technology, and the arts—required the emergence of a new world view or, as it were, a new Turk. The revolutionary image, in its ideal terms, stressed devotion to the nation and its leader, the importance of improving life on this earth, the idea of free individual will, the rationalist approach and the spirit of inquiry, and the recognition of the economic function of the human being stimulated by the state as well as private enterprise. Such a frontal cultural transformation naturally viewed some aspects of Islam as antithetical and even inimical. It found one basic Islamic concept particularly objectionable— submission to one's preordained fate. It identified the fatalism, which had been the unfortunate product of an originally high ethical precept, as the root of such maladies as lethargy, apathy, superstition, despondency, and torpor. It virtually held the Islamic institution responsible for destitution. It assigned to itself the task of removing the self-hate and the *contemptus mundi* that the aberrations of scholasticism had fostered. In its place, the Kemalist doctrine tried to implant self-affirmation and *dignitas homini*.

The ideology implemented in Turkey—referred to as "Kemalism" until the mid-1930s and as "Ataturkism" later—was a unique synthesis which combined selective features of contemporary ideologies. With emphasis on nationalism plus rationalism, it defined its own principles as "republicanism, nationalism, etatism, populism, secularism, and reformism." In its emotional fervor, nationalism seemed to function as the New Religion. Ataturk's secularism strove to give the nation a new ethos invoking the pre-Islamic mythos as well as transposing some traditional Islamic values into a non-religious context. Many intellectuals and educators disseminated the propaganda side of the military triumphs and the "glorious civilization" of the Turks, particularly in Central Asia, their ancestral homeland, with their own deity, the "Tengri" (Sky God), and their mythic heroes. Thus, the Ottoman period, except for its conquering heroes, was shown as only one major segment in a long history of military and cultural achievement. Ataturk (the surname given to him by an act of Parliament means "Father of the Turks" or "Ancestral Father") was, as praised in public statements and in a vast corpus of panegyrics, the manifest destiny of that history and the nation's "eternal chief."

Kemalist secularism seemed aware of the fact that it could not, nor should it attempt to, root out Islam, choosing rather to let a sustained educational process eventually reduce its hold on life and culture. Unlike the neighboring Soviet leadership, it did not preach atheistic materialism. As a deliberate policy, it interpreted laicism (secularism) as making faith a matter of private conscience and keeping organized religion out of government. Ataturk probably knew full well the truth in Edward Gibbon's observation in *The Decline and Fall of the Roman Empire* that "memory of theological opinions cannot long be preserved without the artificial help of priests, of temples, and of books." Individuals were free to pray and engage in the practice of Islam. Significantly, Turkey's third strongest man (after Ataturk and Inonu), Field Marshal Fevzi Cakmak, Chief of the General Staff for nearly twenty years, encompassing the entire presidency of Ataturk, was a devout Moslem who never stopped his religious observances. Abdulhalik Renda, Speaker of the Parliament, was often seen praying in mosques. Turkish secularism was resolved to break sacerdotal power and Islam's emotional and cultural dominion. It respected and officially observed religious holidays. It even tried to make Islam more meaningful, at least rationally intelligible, by having the call to prayer chanted in Turkish and having the Koran translated in its entirety into Turkish, although conservatives claimed that all this was a way of tampering with the sanctity of the Koranic language.

As established governmental principle and policy during the presidencies of Ataturk (1923-38) and of Inonu (1938-50), secularism was confronted with growing opposition, sometimes expressing itself in militant terms. After the establishment of the multi-party system soon after the end of World War II, the burgeoning democratic process, including widening freedoms, stimulated and permitted the revival of religious activities. It was apparent by the late 1960s that not only had mosque attendance increased greatly but also that Islamic sentiments were finding expression in political action.

The revival could be explained in terms of many factors. For one thing, the Ataturk reforms had never really penetrated the rural areas. Secularism was essentially an urban, upper, and middle-class phenomenon. In the small towns and in the 40,000 villages in Anatolia, Islam remained *the* faith. Even in the secular strongholds, there were stirrings for a systematized moral and ethical life. Nationalism no longer provided spiritual satisfaction. Its spellbinding hero was gone. World War II and its aftermath had demonstrated the weaknesses, the depressing vulnerability of Turkey: the myth of Turkish military might had eroded without even being tested by the war. Nationalism, which had based its appeal on that myth, seemed like nothing other than declamatory propaganda. Turkish universities and intellectuals had failed to develop the Ataturk doctrines into a viable substantive program, let alone a full-fledged ideology. Nationalism offered no solution to economic problems and no strategy for living. Islam, at least, gave the "lumpenproletariat" a sanctuary for consolation in this life and the hope of paradise in the next.

Mosque building, which had virtually stopped in the first quarter-century of the Republic, is now a flourishing industry all over Turkey. State TV and radio stations carry many religious programs, particularly during

Ramadan (the month of fasting). In addition to the upsurge in orthodox Islam, a variety of banned brotherhoods—not just the whirling Mevlevi dervishes who have received considerable official support since the mid-1950s—have started to surface, and by the pervasive visibility of Islam are now a fact of Turkish life.

The upsurge, although impressive, has not converted Turkey into an Islamic state. The structure and dynamics of government remain staunchly secular despite pressures from religious groups and their elected representatives. In Turkey, Islam is not the state religion, but the faith of the nation. The system effectively maintains a distinct separation of state and religion. Turkey's vital sectors have modernized. The legal and executive processes remain unaffected in any fundamental sense by the intrusions of religious propaganda. Women's rights and participation in all walks of life are already far ahead of any other Moslem country and compare favorably with virutally all of the developing countries and with many among the developed. Social revolution seems to have outdistanced the inroads made by the Islamic revival. A fundamental goal of the Kemalist transformation—the transition from *tawakkul* (resignation to fate), to *tashabbus* (enterprise and initiative)— has been largely attained. In politics, recent trends have demonstrated that the electorate, which is more than 99 percent Moslem, is not solely motivated by Islam when it comes to voting: the National Salvation Party, which mustered 49 seats out of 450 in the National Assembly in 1973, won only 24 seats in 1977.

Significantly, however, one of the major reasons for the military takeover in September 1980 was the anxiety over the growing threat against secularism which it perceived. Ataturkism, including its secular principles, constitutes the doctrine of the new military regime.

As a matter of historical determinism, Turkey cannot be expected, after a modernization process of nearly 150 years, to revert to an Islamic type of government. The imperatives of Turkish history and the indigenous features of Turkish culture probably obviate desecularization. A scenario comparable to the Ayatollah Khomeini's Iran is unthinkable for Turkey. Only two highly improbable internal developments might tend to give more of a religious reorientiation to the Turkish governmental system: one is the emergence of an extraordinary Islamic leader with a genius for rallyng a massive segment of 50 million Turks around religious causes. The other is a military commander who becomes victorious in a major war, takes over the reins of government, and as a military dictator chooses to accommodate Islam in his policies.

The force of external circumstances does not appear capable of setting Turkey on the road to desecularization. Islam has not yet come into its own as the world's "Third Ideology," nor do the forty Muslim nations constitute a power bloc. In the world of Islam, there are no functional programs of economic and political cooperation let alone military alliance. Arabs and Turks appear to be divided by the same religion. Only if an eruption of the Crusades pits the Muslim world against non-Muslims, Turkey might become part of an Islamo-centrist alignment. Or else it will be necessary for the oil-rich Muslim nations to spend billions in aid and credit for Turkey's economic recovery before Turkey would join an Islamic bloc in active fashion. Even in that case it might avoid making major compromises in its secular system.

Turkish Islam, internally, will no doubt continue to be edifying for millions, but probably not politically unifying. Externally, it is unlikely to make Turkey an active member of an Islamic alliance. Given its enchorial culture, its ancient and modern history, and its own aspirations, it will not be easy, perhaps not even possible, for Turkey to rejoin the mainstream of political Islam.

16

Islam in Modern Indonesia

POLITICAL IMPASSE, CULTURAL OPPORTUNITY

Donald K. Emmerson

IN INDONESIA, ISLAM IS AN ACTIVE MINORITY—within a numerical majority—inside a pluralistic society under an authoritarian government engaged in secular development. Since 1965 to 1967, when Soeharto's New Order replaced Sukarno's Old, these conditions have interacted to thwart Muslim efforts to rule.

Politically enfeebled, Indonesian Islam is still a vigorous culture. In the 1970s, the government has had to respect Muslim sensitivities in matters of family law, interfaith competition, and religious education. But neither side has been able to separate religion from politics.

The generals who run the New Order, many of them only superficially Muslim, see in Islam's cultural strength a political threat. Concessions to Muslim pride are made for security reasons, lest angry believers shake the regime. Organized Muslims, in turn, are unwilling to limit their activity to the nonpolitical realm. This refusal stems not only from adherence to doctrinal principle—the unity of religion and politics in Islam—but also from fear of being cordoned off from the state. Even after years of political defeat, the prospect of legislating the piety of a lax majority remains attractive to many Muslim leaders.

The ambitions of both sides are basically defensive: to protect the transconfessional unity of the nation, on the one hand, and to halt the erosion of its major religion, on the other. But these theoretically compatible aims have become polarized in rhetorical arguments over whether the state should be either secular or Islamic. The government worries that Muslim groups will use their faith to break up the state. Muslim groups fear that the state will be used to break up their faith. By thinking the worst of its opponent, and behaving accordingly, each side unintentionally confirms the suspicion of the other.

In the 1980s, three things could happen. First, by joining the extraparliamentary opposition to what certain retired officers have already begun to describe openly as Soeharto's hypocritical misrule, organized Muslims could hope to be pulled into power in the wake of a coup. Second, Muslim leaders could turn inward, away from political rivalry with outsiders and with each other, in order to raise the religious and social consciousness of their followers. Third, the Islamic community's representatives could continue to vie for offices, seats, and votes, achieving neither the radical legitimacy of noncooperation with an increasingly unpopular regime nor the ability to implement from inside the New Order whatever political goals Islam can be said to have.

In the light of Indonesian conditions, a fourth scenario, in which Islam becomes the sole center of political gravity, seems improbable enough to be ignored, as does a fifth, in which repression and secularization remove the country's practicing Muslims entirely from public life. Admittedly, the backlash from an effort to achieve one of these two extreme opposite results could cause the other to occur. (Officials who would destroy organized Islam, for example, may assure its political future. "Religion is like a nail. The harder you hit it, the deeper it goes into the wood.") But Iran is not the future of Indonesia.

Of the three plausible outcomes, the first is not something Muslim leaders can do much to bring about. An opportunity to share power would most likely arise from an intramilitary split—as happened in 1965 and again, though with far less damage, in 1974. Nor would that opportunity necessarily endure. In a period of normalization following a future coup, Muslim militants could be outmaneuvered—as they were in the late 1960s when the New Order divorced its original allies, and again in 1971 and 1977 when Soeharto's electoral machine rolled over the opposition.

The second strategy, to turn a political retreat into a cultural opportunity, presupposes collective restraint and creative introspection. Among the country's Muslim organizations, one is unlikely to withdraw from political combat and the promise of spoils unless the others are willing to do so, while the risk of apostasy discourages them all from acknowledging Islam as a cultural but not a political force. This option has also been discredited by association with the colonial Islamologist Snouck Hurgronje's attempt to render Muslims in the Indies harmless by allowing them complete freedom to indulge their piety in strictly nonpolitical ways.

Barring a major crisis, the status quo seems likely to continue, at least through the 1982 election. For political Muslims, this third path is the least arduous, for it requires them neither to launch an all-out struggle for full control of the state nor to rethink their rationalizations of Islam's role in the modern world. The rest of this short essay will be spent putting hair on these bald assertions.

Indonesia is the world's largest Islamic society. Almost as many Muslims (some 130 million) can be counted in Indonesia as in its two nearest competitors combined (Pakistan and Bangladesh, with slightly over 70 million apiece). But Indonesia is also the largest archipelagic nation, spanning all or parts of five large and thousands of smaller inhabited islands, each one ecologically and ethnolinguistically distinct. This fragmented setting has thwarted the hopes of religious and political missionaries for ideological purity and uniformity across space and for consistency of belief and behavior over time.

Thus, Muslim leaders who introduced Islam into the archipelago a millennium ago did not represent the first religion to arrive. Hinduism and Buddhism had preceded them. Just as these earlier imports had spread unevenly from culture to culture, alternately mixing and conflicting with each other and with still older, local beliefs and rituals, so did Islam.

Acculturation diversified what being a Muslim could mean. Some definitions dispensed with a boundary between nature and supernature. In Central Java, a fisherman who was Muslim in this sense could propitiate the goddess of the southern seas without feeling even a little heretical. Other renditions incorporated elements of other world religions. In East Java, a mosque was built with wings borrowed from a Hindu mythological bird. Still other versions recognized the opposition as well as the attraction of Muslims to other forms. In West Sumatra, the Minangkabau saying, "religion climbs, custom descends," recapitulates the historical ascent of Islam from the coast towards its encounter with pre-Muslim culture in the highlands. Such meetings were generally peaceful, but not always. On Java, Sumatra, and other islands, irregularly down to the present day, self-consciously Muslim movements have come into varying degrees of conflict with non-Muslim or nominally Muslim aristocratic, ethnic, religious, and political groups.

The latest wave of cultural change, secularization, has also spread unevenly through different hosts. Muslims whose religion was already a secondary aspect of private life were able to adapt, more or less. But those who insisted on preserving Islam's public mission felt threatened, as they had been by colonization and Christianization. In the eyes of many of these misnamed "militants"—a label that imputes aggression not self-defense (and connotes disapproval by tolerant private believers and agnostics)—modernization is another conspiracy of the West.

Had the devout been a great majority, they could have grown an Islamic state in independent Indonesia organically, "from below," by making official what was customary. On the contrary, practicing Muslims were a minority inside a lax or syncretic majority, especially on Java, the new nation's demographic, cultural, and political core. Lacking an effective mass base, Muslim politicians lobbied instead in constituent and consultative assemblies from the 1940s onward, hoping to create an Islamic state artificially by legislative fiat "from above."

They failed. The nominal nature of Indonesia's statistically Muslim majority, the power and fears of Christians and other non-Muslims, and the transconfessional or secular priorities of Sukarno (national unity) and Soeharto (economic growth) all helped to defeat political Islam. Meanwhile, in the provinces, those who sporadically waged holy wars fared no better.

Muslim politicians were not wholly out of power. In the 1950s, during Indonesia's experiment with liberal democracy, they were appointed and elected to office and took part in cabinets and coalitions. They staffed a ministry of religion that had been created in 1946 to reward their support for the revolution then in progress against the Dutch. But these gains coopted and divided political Islam. The ministry became not a salient but an enclave, while political competition among Muslims reinforced theological differences. In the 1960s, under that decade's two varieties of authoritarian rule, these trends continued, despite the punishment and the opportunity, in turn, delivered to Muslim politicians with the proscription of the reformist Islamic Masjumi party in 1960 and the radical secular Communist Party in 1966.

In the 1970s, the balance of power shifted more decisively against Islam. Having together won more than two-fifths of the votes and seats at stake in the 1955 election, Muslim parties saw their combined strength cut almost to a quarter of the votes and seats contested in 1971, a low point from which only marginal recovery proved possible in the election of 1977. On both of the latter occasions, the government's vehicle, Golkar (Golongan Karya or Functional Groups) racked up large majorities.

Among Muslim organizations, this setback was unequally distributed. Chief losers were those who had hoped to reform and reinvigorate their religion, to recenter it in the Koran and the *hadith*, and who had tried through their social organization, Muhammadijah, and political party, Masjumi, to purify Muslim customs and enact Muslim laws.

Sukarno had banned Masjumi in part for its association with a regional rebellion against his regime. After he was replaced, the ban remained, and Soeharto's general cramped an effort to revive the old party under a new name, Parmusi. To swell the government's majority, more than a fifth of the seats in the new parliament would be appointed. Against such pressures, Parmusi could gain only 5 percent of the seats in Parliament in 1972, compared to Masjumi's 22 percent in 1955.

Masjumi's chief Muslim rival, the Nahdlatul Ulama (NU), had been created in 1926 by conservative Islamic scholar-teachers with followings in rural religious schools, in order to counteract the reformist influence of Muhammadijah. More eclectic in matters of religious law than the reformists, more inclined to settle questions by recourse to orthodox commentaries or to custom, and less willing directly to reevaluate the meaning of the Koran or the *hadith* for fear of error, NU in the 1970s became the largest Muslim party, even managing to enlarge marginally its 18 percent share of the 1955 vote.

Nevertheless, NU found its activities curtailed in several ways. In 1971 and 1977, especially in the party's stronghold province of East Java, government officials hindered the NU campaign. Shortly after the 1971 contest, a "religious technocrat" from outside NU was appointed minister of religion, ending the party's control of patronage in that large department. Finally, NU lost its electoral autonomy altogether in 1973, when the four existing Muslim parties were brought together by the regime to constitute a new organization, whose name—the Unity and Development Party (PPP)— neither denoted nor connoted Islam.

From independence up to the 1970s, NU's willingness to cooperate with and share power in whatever government came along earned it a reputation for opportunism. Its virtual ownership of the ministry of religion necessarily implicated the party in a long series of cabinets. Its religious roots lay in the countryside, notably in the Islamic schools in Jombang, East Java, whence most of its leaders came and where, grown old, they represented the conscience of the party. But more in the limelight in the 1950s and 1960s were the party's "secular" spokesmen in Jakarta, busy getting votes, issuing statements, and filling jobs. The more visible NU's compromises, the less so its conscience, and the more limited its appeal to Indonesian Muslims looking for a consistent religious opposition to join.

In this sense, for NU, the virtual disconnection of organized Islam from national government in the 1970s has been a blessing in disguise. With little to do in Jakarta, some of the party's younger leaders returned to Jombang to refresh themselves at the source. In 1980, the last of the party's original founders, the late Kyai Bisri, refused to seek medical treatment in Jakarta and spent only a few days in a hospital in Surabaya, the capital of East Java, lest he be deprived of his wish to die in Jombang. The analogy is inexact, but the distance from Khomeini's Qom to the Shah's Teheran was also more than geographical.

Far from weakening NU's identity, official efforts to limit the party's opportunities to rule reinforced its religious and political legitimacy. The government not only failed in its attempt to prevent the PPP from campaigning in 1977 under the symbol of the *kabah*, the holy shrine of Islam in Mecca toward which Muslims turn to pray, but the publicity surrounding the attempt reinforced the party's religious legitimacy. In the same election, in ostensibly secular metropolitan Jakarta, the PPP received more votes than Golkar. Apart from its religious reputation, the Islamic party appealed to disenchanted urbanites who saw in it the only significant opposition to repressive, corrupt, inegalitarian rule. Ironically, the generals themselves had cut down NU's competition, by destroying the Communist Party, by not rehabilitating Masjumi, and by undermining the non-Muslim parties' previous support, especially among civil servants beholden to their superiors. Largely for the last reason, for example, the nonconfessional Indonesian National Party, which had outpolled even Masjumi in 1955, collapsed in 1971 to a fraction of its former self.

Despite its popularity, the PPP will almost certainly not replace Soeharto's government by winning an election. Even if, by some stretch of the imagination, the party won all the elected seats in Parliament, it could still turn out to be a minority in the much larger consultative assembly that selects the president, for only two-fifths of the assembly's members are elected. The government appoints the rest. That the PPP could acquire even a majority of the elected seats seems unlikely.

Even in 1977, the PPP won less than 30 percent of the vote. Many nominal Muslims, including students and professional people, voted for the PPP not because they wanted it to run the country, but because through it they could express opposition to the existing regime. The PPP is just the right size to attract this kind of negative support. It is big enough to register the desired impression on the authorities (an effect that ballots cast for the anemic Christian-nationalist opposition would not have), yet small enough to forestall the kind of theocratic success that such relatively secularized urban protest voters could not accept.

Finally, the PPP is not a unified force. Whenever the issue of allocating seats among its constituent organizations arises, old differences reappear. Nor has the government been reluctant to use those differences to its own ends. It is no coincidence that the general chairmen of the PPP have been moderates of proven sympathy to the regime—men disinclined to resurrect Masjumi, unwilling to press for an Islamic state, and set apart by their urbane manner from the simple-living elders of Jombang. For all these reasons, the possibility of an elected PPP government seems remote.

Equally unlikely to be performed in Indonesia is an "Iranian" script in which Islam obtains full power through extralegal means. Indonesia is even more multicultural than Iran. Compared to Iran, Indonesia's much larger size, more dispersed and fragmented physiography, proportionally larger and more influential Christian minorities, Hindu-Buddhist heritage, and greater distance from the heartland of Islam all diminish the prospect that religious revolution will sweep the archipelago.

Additional differences between Iran and Indonesia are worth pointing out. Although the cockpit politics of both Teheran and Jakarta have had dramatic national effects, the Iranian capital is even more of a primate city than its Indonesian counterpart. The greater proportional concentration of population in Teheran makes demonstrations there potentially more consequential.

More important, while limiting the political power of Islam, the military managers of the New Order have been careful not to offend Muslim sensibilities too much. In 1973, army leaders agreed to amend a draft law on marriage in deference to the objections of Muslims that Islamic laws and courts were being ignored. This compromise enabled the government to avoid having to defend itself on two fronts when student demonstrations on secular issues led to mob violence in Jakarta early in 1974.

Other concessions followed. In 1976, Indonesia's attorney general outlawed the Jehovah's Witnesses, whose aggressive evangelism had become notorious among devout Muslims. In 1977, the PPP was allowed to campaign under the sign of the *kabah*. In 1978, over the objection of Christian leaders and their Western missionary supporters, the minister of religion (a general) prohibited the proselytizing of Indonesians who already belonged to a faith, brought foreign aid to religious institutions under closer government control, and instructed those institutions to replace foreign personnel with Indonesians within two years.

In 1979, to the further relief of Islam's defenders, certain mystical "streams of belief," popular among Java's syncretically "Muslim" majority but anathema to devoutly orthodox Muslims, were not given the status of a major new creed in the ministry of religion, but were declared mere folkways and assigned to the ministry of education and culture. Other steps taken by officials in the 1970s to appease Muslim groups included a successful recommendation to the Indonesian Council of Churches not to host a world assembly of Christians and the banning of an annual Christian festival of charity. In the latter case, Islamic leaders feared that the promise of free food and clothing might entice thousands of poor Muslims to abandon their religion. Significantly, both events would have been held in the volatile metropolis, Jakarta. All of these concessions to Muslim pride and sensitivity in the 1970s reflect Soeharto's unwillingness to challenge, or at least to appear to challenge, Islam on spiritual grounds.

That unwillingness leads one to doubt the likelihood of an official assault on organized Islam in the early 1980s. Reportedly, a semiofficial think tank has advised the government to replace religious with ethical instruction in the schools, downgrade the Ministry of Religion to a directorate general within the Ministry of Social Affairs, and proscribe all political parties based on religion—and to render palatable such a drastic separation of state and mosque by building one of the latter in each provincial capital. But recommendations like these seem unlikely to gain acceptance, at least not before the 1982 election, by a government that knows it is not strong enough to risk appearing so transparently hostile to Islam. Already, for this reason, a proposal to replace religious curricula in public schools with courses on comparative religion has been turned down.

As these cases suggest, pluralism exists to a modest degree within the regime. For convenience, I have referred to the "government" and personified it as "Soeharto's," but authority in the New Order is neither fully institutionalized nor limited to the personality of one man. Nor is it a purely military affair; witness the role of civilian technocrats in economic policy making. Nevertheless, when it comes to security, stability, and succession, or whenever an otherwise minor issue can be cast in these terms, army officers make the decisions. This means that a more or less extralegal intramilitary shift, which observers might or might not call a coup, could change the government without changing the regime.

From such an eventuality, Muslim groups could gain in the short run. Should dissident officers decide to move against Soeharto's leadership, they will recognize in political Islam, the country's only organized nationwide opposition, a potential ally. Conversely, Muslim leaders are aware of the presence among active and retired military men of individuals who are both critical of the president and sympathetic to Islam.

In the past, the cross-cutting nature of political controversies in Indonesia's multicultural society limited the prospect of such an alliance. Even today, traditional Muslims, modern students, and professional officers, to repeat the stereotypes, seem unlikely partners in political action. In the future, however, temporary cooperation among these groups will grow less unlikely the more they come to share the same reasons to criticize the government—for engendering massive corruption, violating human rights, undercutting indigenous entrepreneurs, playing religious favorites, enriching the rich while ignoring the poor, encouraging immorality and secular values, and mortgaging the nation's future to world capitalism, to cite recent accusations.

All the same, the chance of political Islam's acquiring power, thanks to such cooperation, should not be overdrawn. To illustrate: the March 1980 issue of Indonesia's largest circulation Muslim magazine featured a retired army general on its cover and reprinted a long interview in which he appeared to suggest that in order to restore a balance of power between civilian and military elements, officers on activity duty should be forbidden to engage in politics. Students too have criticized the armed forces' politico-military role. But the temptation to infer from this apparent convergence of interests an antigovernment alliance of army elements, Muslim leaders, and student radicals should be resisted. The ex-general in question was instrumental in the compromise that allayed Muslim fears at the eleventh hour in the marriage law crisis of 1973. But he played a conciliatory role at that time because he wanted Islam to rule. On the contrary, by defusing Muslim resentments he hoped to save the government from a possibly fatal combination of religious and student radicalism. As for appealing to other grievances, while in office he kept a reputation for being uncorrupt. But, his last job, running special security, implicated him more in the transgression than the defense of human rights.

Nor should one infer from criticism of an incumbent the desire to replace him. In May 1980, fifty Indonesians signed a petition protesting the President's use of the national emblem (Panjasila) to defend himself and his family against rumors of corruption. Among the signatories were several retired officers and ex-Masjumi leaders. But these were critics, not usurpers; they merely wanted Parliament to debate the matter. More dangerous to Soeharto's presidency than the expression of discontent through such "normal channels" are the otherwise implausible coalitions of shared frustration that seem likely to form in the absence of official self-correction, or in the presence of official overreaction to legitimate dissent. Even in an undemocratic regime, interviews and petitions that are brushed aside today can turn out tomorrow to have been straws in a wind of change.

If Indonesia's top rulers are disinclined to engage in self-criticism or thoroughgoing reform, the indications that Muslim leaders will do so are not much better. The cultural defensiveness of Islam in Indonesia, perhaps not unlike the political defensiveness of Soeharto's presidency, has helped to make public discourse rhetorical and self-serving. The more people feel their motives being impugned by others, the less they will question those motives themselves to avoid arming their enemies.

For political Islam, this may be the most debilitating legacy of Indonesia's cultural pluralism and colonial experience. So long as practicing Muslims remain a qualitative minority in a statistical majority, in a diverse society, in a fragmented environment, the temptation to enforce piety from the "top down" will remain. And because of those very conditions, non- and nominal Muslims will continue to fear that "political solution."

Can these mirrors of distrust be broken? Some observers have argued that Muslim leaders should make a cultural virtue of the necessity of political retreat, first, by strengthening, from the "bottom up," the piety of the base on which their long-run political strength must rest, and second, by rethinking the role of Islam in the modern world, so that whenever they reenter the political fray they can do so unburdened by obsolete beliefs and unrealistic expectations.

Unfortunately, the very terms in which this "cultural solution" is expressed make it unacceptable to a Muslim who denies any distinction between politics and religion. My own guess is that this quality of comprehensiveness—the refusal to allocate anything to Caesar alone, upon which so many Western renditions of Islam insist—is not so much doctrinally fixed for all times and places as it is a historical response to adversities such as cultural pluralism and colonial rule. When Muslim partisans stigmatize Golkar as Golkur (Golongan Kuraish) in reference to the idolatrous tribe that surrounded Muhammad in Arabia, or when they discredit the "cultural solution" by associating it with Snouck Hurgronje's wish to domesticate Islam in the Indies, they invoke not the unalterable essence of their religion but its historical experience, whose "essence" was and remains contingency and change. Or so it seems to me.

The behavior of all of us is more or less inconsistent with our actual beliefs, let alone the writing on the banners under which we march. The less we have to march at all, against one or another foe, the easier it will be for us to recognize in our discrepancies not errors to be erased but possible instances of creative adaptation to a changing world. Islam in Indonesia badly needs a period of calm in which such realizations can be made.

Unfortunately, given the unease of the authorities and the proximity of the 1982 election, such introspections will probably continue to be postponed by all parties to an increasingly fragile status quo.

17

Observations on Contemporary Islam

EPILOGUE

Willem Bijlefeld

T IS DIFFICULT TO DO JUSTICE to the cultural diversity and the religious unity of the Muslim world. At the same time, it is a serious distortion to suggest that until very recently the Muslim world was treated everywhere in the West as a monolith. From early in this century onward, American universities have developed area studies programs which so emphasized the local, the national, and the regional manifestations of the Muslim world that the issue of religious unity generally was not even raised. The emphasis thus was on the variety and diversity of the Muslim world rather than on its unity. There has also been, in academic courses and in handbooks on world religions, a focus, at least until the late 1950s, on Islam as *distinct* from the Muslim world, i.e., on Islam as a monolithic system. This focus over-emphasized Islam's classical period and its formal expressions and paid little attention to the lives of hundreds of millions of fellow citizens on this planet.

This emphasis is not an academic question. The issue is whether we can distill common elements from the great variety of regional manifestations in the Muslim world. Can we reconstruct the unity of Islam out of a study of the multiformity and plurality of regional manifestations or should we start with the message of the Holy Koran and the Prophet and then move to see how this message is implemented and manifested under different conditions? If we were to write a book, which still needs to be written, that would convey to American audiences what Islam means, would we start with the diversity of

Islam and then try to distill the common elements or would we start with Islam as an entity and then move to the plurality of its manifestations?

This is a basic question. Many Muslims object to such expressions as "Indonesian Islam." Obviously there are Indonesian Muslims, but what is "Indonesian Islam?" There are Muslims in sub-Saharan Africa but are we justified in talking about African Islam? A great, imaginative Muslim from West Africa once wrote that Islam is like crystal clear water that is so clear that we see the diverse colors of the soil over which the water is running wherever it goes. How can we describe the clarity of that water if it is only the soil that gives it color?

We are often reminded of the necessity to distinguish between Islam and what Muslims make of it. Is Islam, beyond what Muslims make of it, an abstraction, or can we come to terms with it and describe it? No matter which language we use, we must begin to distinguish far more clearly than we have in the past between what is Islamic and what is Muslim. Turkey, for example, is a nation of Muslims, but it is not an Islamic nation. Is it possible for us to find greater clarity on the issue of diversity in unity by distinguishing between the customs and practices of Muslims and Islamic principles? In addition to thinking about cultural diversity, to what extend do we also have to think about religious diversity? Is Islam the singular, and the Muslim world, with all its variety of manifestations, the plural?

Diversity there is, to be sure. There are what we call sects, but let us not fall into the error of treating Sunni and Shii Islam as the two major sects of Islam. Many Christians would be greatly distressed to hear someone referring to His Holiness the Pope as the head of a Christian sect. By the same reasoning, we should not use sectarian language to describe the two branches of Islam. But how much of this is Islamic pluralism and contrary to the unity of faith? There is an endless diversity of social, economic, and political conditions in the Muslim world, but should we call these variations an Islamic diversity? There are also differences in historical context and in character, but why should we describe these as diversity of Islam?

There is a diversity of human beings among Muslims; there are differences between hope and frustration, between confidence and anxiety, between bright and dim prospects for the future, between gratitude for the accomplishments of the recent past and bewilderment by the burden of it. But why are all these differences interpreted as Islamic differences? We recognize that Islam is a totality. Having said that, however, we may fall victims to exaggeration: having comprehended the all-embracing nature of Islam, we try to interpret events in the Muslim world in Islamic terms. When we find that Muslim leaders differ sharply on a particular political issue, why do we go back to the ways in which Islam is meaningful to them to try to explain the difference?

What, in short, gives us the right to interpret the variety of reactions in the Muslim world as Islamic varieties? How much of this reaction can be traced to Islam, and how much needs to be understood and evaluated on non-Islamic terms?

Once again, we introduce normative judgments about who is and who is not a "good" Muslim. What gives us the right to determine what is truly Islamic? But there is a way of coming to terms with the unity of Islam. This unity clearly lies in a single event—the ongoing event of the Holy Koran. There is the enormous impact of Arabic as the liturgical language. There is the singular life of the Prophet Muhammad. There are the ritual daily prayers as an expression of unity and the pilgrimage to Mecca.

There are two other notions. One is our need to recognize the Muslim acknowledgement of the unity of humankind. In one of the most astounding surahs of the Koran, Surah 30, there is the statement not that Islam meets human needs or that it is in line with human character, but that, by the grace of God, human nature is in accord with Islam. Whatever the diversity of cultures, of political situations, of backgrounds, and of historical experience, we all have one thing in common: "our humaness." This is not only one of the most distinctive contributions of Islam to the unity of the Muslim community, it also builds bridges beyond the Muslim community. After all, what we have in common is our common humanity. And there is a mysterious but real unity in that.

The other notion is the unity of God and the singularity of our response to it. Islam does not mean passive resignation. Islam, after all, is the only religion whose name is an active participle. Islam stands for an outburst of action, an unquestioning commitment to the one and only God and to His will. Whatever else Islam is, it is a call to obedience to God. Indeed, in that sense, Islam rules out a plurality. There is no god but God, there is nothing that can claim our ultimate loyalty except the ultimate truth of God Himself. That is obedience, but it is more than passive obedience. The unity of Islam is anchored in a Muslim awareness of the sufficiency of God. Whatever our deficiencies, whatever we fail to make of the will of God, whatever the shortcomings, whatever the fears, frustrations, anxieties, and uncertainties, "Our sufficiency is God." Perhaps it is in that rich but simple Koranic expression, more than in anything else, that we can begin to have a taste of what the unity of Islam—as faith, as commitment, as promise, and as assurance—really is.

Glossary

ARABIC IS THE LANGUAGE OF ISLAM, even though Muslims speak many different languages. Islamic terms, therefore, are generally Arabic or derived from Arabic. There is considerable variation, however, in the pronunciation of Islamic terms among non-Arabic speaking societies. Transliteration into the Latin alphabet tends to vary with the writer. For this book, the editors have tried to standardize the spelling of the terms listed in this glossary, but there will be variants, especially in less frequently used terms. We have used the spellings found in many American dictionaries for such relatively common terms as Koran, *muezzin*, and *ulema*.

Allah	the Arabic name for God used by all Muslims and by Arabic-speaking Christians
ayatollah	(Persian) literally reflection or symbol of God; used specifically to refer to Iranian religious leaders
dar al-Islam	the Muslim world; lands under Muslim rule or lands in which Muslim institutions are maintained; literally "house of Islam"
dar al-Harb	the non-Muslim world, lands in which Muslim institutions do not prevail; literally "house of war"
fiqh	the science of Islamic law or jurisprudence. Of the various schools or rites of jurisprudence that arose among sunni Muslims, four are considered orthodox: *Hanafi, Maliki, Shafii*, and *Hanbali*. About half of the sunnis adhere to the Hanafi school. The conservative Hanbali school is the smallest; its stronghold is Saudi Arabia

hadith	the mass of religious traditions; the record of an act or saying or decision of the Prophet, his Companions and accredited successors as established by the consensus (*ijma*) of the *ulema*; the *hadith*, together with the Koran, provide the foundation of theology and law
hajj	the pilgrimage to Mecca in the last month of the Muslim calendar; required of a Muslim at least once in a lifetime (one of the five obligatory duties)
haram	taboo, forbidden, sacrosanct, especially the Holy Places in Mecca and Medina and the sanctuaries in Jerusalem, Karbala, and elsewhere; also used for the women's quarters of a house (harem)
ijma	consensus (of the *ulema*); the collective opinion of those learned in the law; a major source of Islamic law
itjihad	interpretation; reasoning by analogy; interpreting the Koran and the sunnah; the exercise of indepdendent judgment in deriving rules of conduct from the sources of Islamic law and jurisprudence
imam	a leader, particularly of public prayer and by extension of the Muslim community; among shii Muslims, the term connotes considerable spiritual authority
Islam	submission to the will of God; used in reference to the community of believers and their faith
jihad	literally a striving or a struggling; usually applied to holy war against unbelievers in accordance with Islamic law but also refers to a believer's struggle in the path of God against base impulses, injustices, etc. (a fighter in a *jihad* is a *mujahid*)
Koran	(Quran) the book of "recitations" of the word of God as revealed to the Prophet Mohammad; the holy book of Islam; contains about 6000 verses and 114 chapters (surahs)
madrasah	seminary or academy for Muslim learning
mufti	a specialist in Muslim law; authority originally derived from his own scholarly reputation; rulers later appointed official muftis from the ranks of scholars; the ruling or opinion a mufti issues on a point of law is called a *fatwa*
Muhammad	(A.D. 570-632) the Prophet or Messenger of God who received God's word as contained in the Koran
mullah	a religious teacher; preacher
Muslim	(Moslem) a person who submits to the will of God; an adherent of Islam
qadi	a judge who administers Islamic law
shahadah	the profession of faith; "There is no God but God; Muhammad is the Messenger of God"

shariah	the Holy Law of Islam; the body of rules governing the life of a Muslim; legal doctrine derived from the Koran and the sunnah; the totality of God's commandments as revealed in the Koran and elaborated in the *hadith*
shiah	(shiite; shii; shiis) "partisans of Ali"; the branch of Islam whose adherents hold that the succession to Muhammad should have been through Ali, Muhammad's cousin and son-in-law, and Ali's descendants; developed into a religious movement in the early centuries of Islam; differs from Sunni Islam on various points of doctrine and law; now found principally in Iran, Iraq, and Yemen, but also in Afghanistan and Pakistan; about 14 percent of Muslims are shii
shirk	the worst and only unpardonable sin; joining or associating other gods with the one true God; polytheism
sufi; sufism	the form that mysticism has taken in Islam; a mode of thinking and feeling; often organized in fraternities, orders, or brotherhoods, e.g., the Qadiris, Naqshabandis, Mevlevis, Bektashis
sunnah	the accepted practice and belief of the Muslim community, based on the precedents of the Prophet; next to the Koran, the most important doctrinal source
sunni	(sunnite; sunnis) a follower of the tradition; loosely translated as "orthodox"; a Muslim belonging to the majority branch of Islam whose adherents believed that Muhammad's successor as head of the Muslim community should have been, as he was, elected from among the Companions of the Prophet; now comprises about 85 percent of all Muslims
surah	a chapter of the Koran; they are arranged, except for the first, in order of length
tariqah	(plu. *tariqat*) sufi fraternity or order; religious brotherhood
ulema	(*ulama*) the class of professional men learned in the law and religious studies who form the nearest Muslim equivalent to a clergy; (sing. *alim*)
ummah	the religious-political community of Islam; also used for non-Muslim communities—Christians, Jews
waqf	an endowment or trust of land or other property that produces income; the income may be assigned such institutions as a mosque or a school, or to the founder's family
zakah	a tithe or alms tax; one of the five obligatory duties of a Muslim; the five "pillars" of Islam

Selected Bibliography

T HE WORKS LISTED HERE REPRESENT A SMALL SAMPLING of the literature. They will serve to inform the interested non-specialist about the historical and cultural dimensions of Islam as well as its more purely religious aspect.

Specific subjects are addressed in the *Encyclopedia of Islam*. The old edition of 1913 is being superceded by a new edition, an international enterprise incorporating contributions by leading scholars and requiring decades to complete. Headings through the letter K are now published in volumes available in public and university libraries.

Ali, Abdullah Yusif. *The Holy Qur'an: Text, Translation and Commentary.* Washington, D.C.: The American International Printing Co., 1946, xx + 1862 pages. Still widely available, this is a useful translation with parallel texts in Arabic and English and extensive explanatory notes.

Asad, Muhammad. *The Message of the Qur'an*, Translated and Explained. Gibraltar: Dar al-Andalus; Leiden and London: E.J. Brill, 1980. x + 998 pages. A life work of scholarship presenting a thoughtful English translation of the Koran in parallel columns with the Arabic text.

Craig, Kenneth, and Marston Speight. *Islam from Within: Anthology of a Religion.* Belmont, Calif.: Wadsworth, 1980. Paperback. Part of the *Religious Life of Man* series, this is a useful selection of writings of Muslims on Islam. It covers theological, legal, artistic and other dimensions of Islamic civilization and leading contemporary issues of a political and social nature.

Esposito, John L., ed. *Islam and Development: Religion and Sociopolitical Change.* Syracuse: Syracuse University Press, 1980. xx + 268 pages. A collection of essays by specialists countering the prevalent assumption in much social science literature that religion, in general, and Islam, in particular, are obstacles to development. Available in paperback.

Fernea, Elizabeth, and B. Q. Bezirgan, eds. *Middle Eastern Muslim Women Speak.* Austin: University of Texas Press, 1977. Paperback. A collection of historical and contemporary statements by and about Muslim women.

Geertz, Clifford. *Islam Observed: Religious Development in Morocco and Indonesia.* Chicago: University of Chicago Press, 1968. Paperback. A path-breaking study of Islam in its contrasting Asian and North African settings by an outstanding anthropologist.

Hitti, Philip K. *Islam: A Way of Life.* Minneapolis: University of Minnesota Press, 1974. Paperback. A useful introduction that provides historical background and an examination of Islam as religion and culture.

Hodgson, Marshal G. S. *The Venture of Islam: Conscience and History in a World Civilization.* 3 vols. Chicago: University of Chicago Press, 1974. Paperback. A work of profound scholarship. The thirty-page epilogue in vol. 3, "The Islamic Heritage and the Modern Conscience," is especially worth reading.

Kramer, Martin. *Political Islam.* The Washington Papers, vol. 8, no. 73. Beverly Hills and London: Sage Publications, 1980. An excellent, brief analytical survey of the way in which Islam influences the domestic and external politics of Muslim countries.

Kritzeck, James, ed. *Anthology of Islamic Literature.* New York: Mentor, 1966. Paperback. Translation of selections from the Arabic, Persian, and Turkish literary traditions from the rise of Islam to the modern era.

———. *Modern Islamic Literature.* New York: Mentor, 1970. Paperback. A broad selection of writings, including poetry, from 1800 to the present.

Lewis, Bernard, ed. and trans. *Islam, From the Prophet Muhammad to the Culture of Constantinople.* Vol. 1, *Politics and War.* Vol. II, *Religion and Society.* New York: Harper and Row, 1975. Paperback. A documentary history of Islam over its first eight centuries, with materials illustrating different facets of Muslim life and culture.

Pullapilly, Cyril K., ed. *Islam in the Contemporary World.* Notre Dame: Cross Roads Books, 1980.

Rahman, Fazlur, *Islam*, 2nd ed. Chicago: University of Chicago Press, 1979. Paperback. A superb introduction to the development of Islam through fourteen centuries, with an epilogue discussing the significance and implications of events of the past few years for the future of Islam.

Rice, David Talbot. *Islamic Art.* New York: Praeger, 1965. Paperback. A good introduction to the subject with fine illustrations.

Rodinson, Maxime. *Mohammed.* Translated by Anne Carter. New York: Vintage Books, 1974. xx + 361 pages. Paperback. An important work by a leading French scholar who attempts to bring new understanding to the life of the Prophet and the birth of Islam by focusing attention on the person and family circumstances of the young Mohammed and on the socioeconomic milieu of Mecca in his time.

Savory, R. M., ed. *Introduction to Islamic Civilization.* New York: Cambridge University Press, 1976. Paperback. A good collection of essays ranging over aspects of Islamic civilization and its relations with the non-Muslim world.

Schacht, Joseph, and C. E. Bosworth, eds. *The Legacy of Islam.* 2nd ed. Oxford: The Clarenden Press, 1979. Paperback. Contributions by leading scholars on aspects of Muslim civilization, understood broadly in geographic and thematic terms. Of special interest is the first essay, "The Western Image and Western Studies of Islam," by Maxime Rodinson.

Watt, W. Montgomery. *Bell's Introduction to the Qur'an.* Chicago: Aldine, 1970. The best introduction among several English language presentations of the Koran.

_____. *Muhammad, Prophet and Statesman.* Oxford: Oxford University Press, 1974. Paperback. A standard modern biography, one of several now available.

Williams, John Alden. *Islam.* New York: Washington Square Press, 1964. A good, standard study, looking at Islam past and present as a religiously integrated way of life.

Index

CHANGE AND THE MUSLIM WORLD

was composed in 10-point Compugraphic Times Roman and leaded two points
by Emerald Graphics,
with photo display type in Rondo by J.M. Bundscho, Inc.;
printed on 55-pound acid-free Glatfelter Antique Cream,
adhesive-bound with Corvon 22-13 covers, printed by Frank A. West Co.,
by Maple-Vail Book Manufacturing Group, Inc.;
and published by

SYRACUSE UNIVERSITY PRESS

SYRACUSE, NEW YORK 13210